INTO JAPAN

John Lowe

JOHN MURRAY

For Susan

With love and admiration

© John Lowe 1985

First published 1985
by John Murray (Publishers) Ltd
50 Albemarle Street, London W1X 4BD

Paperback edition 1986

Typeset by Inforum Ltd, Portsmouth
Printed and bound in Great Britain
by the Bath Press, Avon

British Library CIP Data
Lowe, John, *1928–*
Into Japan.
1. Japan—Description and travel—1945–
I. Title
915.2′0448   DS811
ISBN 0–7195–4320–7

Into Japan

Into Japan provides an excellent introduction for the intending visitor, the armchair traveller, and the growing number of foreign businessmen and women who go to work in Japan. Whatever subject it touches – cabarets, commerce or Confucianism – is brought to life by the day-to-day experiences of the author, who has felt some of the severe pressures of this overcrowded country and struggled to sort out the enigmas of the Japanese people, so different from the rest of the world.

Japan has been misrepresented and misunderstood in the Western world since it reopened its doors, closed for 215 years, in the middle of the nineteenth century; the country has been sentimentalised by early visitors and writers and, more recently, vilified by frustrated businessmen and perplexed politicians. As the author takes us through Japan, places and experiences in each area highlight different elements of Japanese life and illustrate the strengths and weaknesses of this distinctive society.

John Lowe first went to Japan in 1967 to organise an exhibition of Queen Victoria's coronation robes in Tokyo. He then visited Japan each year, working as a consultant for various Japanese companies, organising cultural tours for British and American tourists, and writing articles and lecturing about Japan. He has travelled all over Japan, made an extensive study of Japanese traditional crafts, which was the subject of his last book (1983), and had a variety of Japanese experiences including living for a short while as a Zen monk.

Contents

Illustrations

All photographs by the author, except 2, 6 and 22 by courtesy of the Japan Information Centre, London

Acknowledgements

Most journeys are only as good as the companions one shares them with. My first view of the Acropolis was turned to dross by the head of an Oxford college who threw a pedagogic shroud over it. But there have been strolls with friends to the most mundane destinations which have turned into odysseys. This book is the story of a journey stretching over eighteen years. If there is some concoction in the itinerary and a certain tampering with the time machine, my companions are real enough. Of various nationalities, many professions and varied interests, each of them added to my pleasure and my understanding, by their own knowledge and enthusiasms.

To some I owe a special debt of gratitude. I would like to thank my children, Judith, Mark and Dominic, for coming to live through long, hot summers in an extremely small Kyoto apartment. It was a test of forbearance which taught us something about the modern Japanese way of life, and perhaps something about ourselves.

At the beginning I owed my introduction to Japan to Seibu Ltd and the kindness of my colleagues in that company, particularly Takao Mori and Shigeo Tanaka. Since then, so many Japanese friends, acquaintances and colleagues have helped me, it is possible to list them by name only without describing their particular contributions. I express my warmest thanks to Kenichi Kinokuni, K. Oda, Mikiko Toda, Akiko Ishijima, Tsune Sesoko, Kyo Ishizaki, Shige Morishita and all his family, Fumio Watanabe, Yoshikazu Takahashi, Tomoko Abe, Harumi Isobe, Hitomi Okamura, Kaoru and Misako Imanishi and Eu-chan, Haruji Nakamura, Masaoki and Junko Takahashi, Nadeshiko Yamaguchi, Kimikazu Kamei, Ishinosuki Mizutani and all his family, Hisako Itoh, Ikuyo Iio, Haruo and Yuko Morishita, Soheku

Acknowledgements

Ogata and her son, Takako Yamana, Takashi Yanagi, and the Nagatani family who run one of the best Chinese restaurants in Kyoto.

There was a memorable month I spent in Kyoto with the late Philip Hofer, notable American book collector. There was a month working on some design seminars with Roger Nicholson. There were sixty-five British and Americans I guided around Japan on three cultural tours, some of them old friends. And since I have lived here, there have been many visitors who either shared brief journeys or taught me from their own travels. I am grateful to Jeff Lowe, Feliciano Bejar, Hans Schneider, Garrick Davis and several others. I am also indebted to Brian Howard and Peter Spriddell of Marks & Spencer who invited me to join them for a week in a fascinating investigation of Japanese shopping.

At various times I have received help and encouragement from many people in Japan and elsewhere, among them Sir John Pilcher, Peter Martin, Lois Karhu, Steve Addiss, Alex and Cally Cochran, David Crane, Otis and Alice Cary, Eilene Kovell, Lars Holmstrom, John Mosher, Peter O'Connell, Christopher Purvis, Bob Sawers, Brian Williams, and from that admirable newspaper, the *Japan Times*. To my editor, Duncan McAra, warmest thanks for his patience and valuable advice.

Finally, a special word of thanks to Yukiko Nomura, who not only organised my tour of Chugoku, but who patiently looked after me while I was writing this book and kindly drew the maps, checked my Japanese spelling and advised me on important points of Japanese life and language. Japan, whether you are travelling about it, or writing about it, is a confusing place. I should have been lost without her help.

This book is based largely on personal experiences. However, I have read a great deal about Japan and would not have been able to interpret those experiences without the help of the books that have taught me so much. The short reading list at the end of this book does not demonstrate my enormous debt to other writers on Japan; that list is deliberately selective and aimed at the general reader, and includes a few books which might be ignored by the scholar but which seem to me to give an insight about day-to-day Japanese life.

As far as possible I have avoided the use of Japanese words. Where I have been forced to use a Japanese word because it is not translatable, I have tried to make the meaning clear by the context, and the words are included in the index with a translation. Much of this book is autobiographical. Where I thought I might cause embarrassment, I have altered names and, on occasions, places. Japanese names are given in the western order, first name followed by family name. In all Japanese words I have omitted accents on the long vowels but otherwise have followed the Hepburn system of spelling.

J.L.

Kyoto, 1984

The Main Periods of Japanese History

Jomon–200 BC
Yayoi 200 BC–AD 250
Kofun 250–552
Asuka 552–645
Nara 645–794
Heian 794–1185
Kamakura 1185–1392
Muromachi 1392–1568
Momoyama 1568–1600
Edo 1600–1868
Meiji 1868–1912
Taisho 1912–1926
Showa 1926–the present

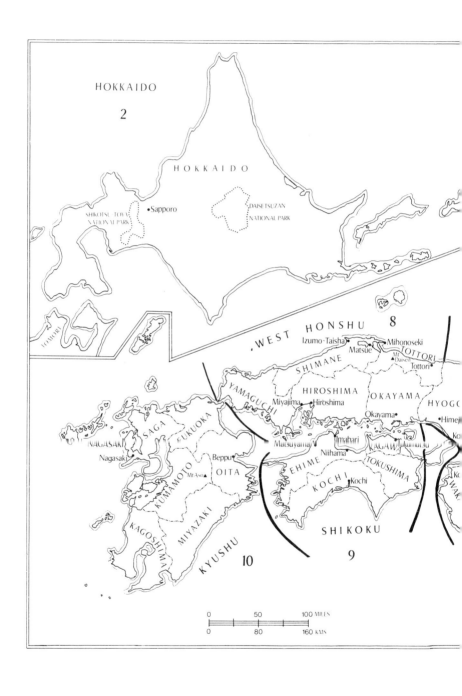

HOKKAIDO

2

HOKKAIDO

SHIKOTSU-TOYA
NATIONAL PARK

•Sapporo

DAISETSUZAN
NATIONAL PARK

TOMORI

•WEST HONSHU

8

Izumo-Taisha•   •Mihonoseki
          Matsue•   TOTTORI
SHIMANE   ▲Mt.
                     Daisen   Tottori•

YAMAGUCHI   HIROSHIMA   OKAYAMA   HYOGO
           Miyajima• •Hiroshima
                              Okayama•   •Hime
SAGA   FUKUOKA   Ko
NAGASAKI   •Matsuyama   Imabari•   KAGAWA Takamatsu•
Nagasaki•   Beppu•   •Niihama   TOKUSHIMA   Ko
        KUMAMOTO Mt.Aso▲ OITA   EHIME   Ko
                 MIYAZAKI   KOCHI   •Kochi   WA
KAGOSHIMA
                          KYUSHU   SHIKOKU
                            10   9

0   50   100 MILES
0   80   160 KMS

N

2

HOKKAIDO

AOMORI

•Aomori

3

•Akita

AKITA

•Morioka

IWATE

Miyako•

•Hiraizumi

SEA OF JAPAN

SADO
ISLAND

4

YAMAGATA

MIYAGI

RIKUCHU KAIGAN NATIONAL PARK

5

•Niigata

•Yamagata

•Sendai

NORTH HONSHU

ISHIKAWA

TOYAMA

•Toyama

NIIGATA

FUKUSHIMA

•Kanazawa

Nagano•

NGO
ULA

hashidate

FUKUI

Takayama•

GUMMA

•Nikko

TOCHI

Matsumoto•

•Mashiko

LHIGA

Lake
Biwa

GIFU

NAGANO

SAITAMA

IBARAKI

IA

•Gifu

•Nagoya

YAMANASHI

TOKYO

HI

AICHI

Mt Fuji▲

Yokohama•

•Tokyo

CHIBA

EAST CENTRAL HONSHU

KAGOSHIMA

MIE

Ise•

SHIZUOKA

Hakone

KANAGAWA

•Toba

•Kamakura

ENTRAL HONSHU

10

OKINAWA

0   100   200 MILES

0   160   320 KMS

Introduction

For several years, due to its enviable economic success, Japan has been under international scrutiny. Around the world, economists pore over the statistics, management consultants dissect commercial structures, while sociologists peer eagerly into each corner of the Japanese social system. Matching these professional studies, a growing international curiosity has led to a proliferation of art exhibitions, Japanese shops and restaurants in major cities everywhere. In the United States and Europe, garden clubs and other earnest groups apply themselves to flower arrangement, tea ceremony or Zen meditation. At the same time international press and television tend to foster an exotic image which too often has little to do with the realities of modern Japan. Seldom was a small country so envied, with growing signs of alarm; seldom was a country, so crucial to the future of the world, so little understood.

There are two main reasons for this ignorance. First, because of its extraordinary differences, Japan is not an easy country to understand. Second, and closely related to the first reason, the Japanese are inept at explaining themselves to other people. They are bad at being objective about themselves. They do not really wish others to understand them. Even more, most Japanese people sincerely believe that foreigners are incapable of understanding them. This attitude is shown by the fact that Japanese people believe that only they can speak true Japanese, which they call *kokugo*. Those not born Japanese can speak only a different kind of Japanese, called *nihongo*. To the Japanese, even a foreigner born and brought up in Japan, going through the complete Japanese educational system from kindergarten to university, will still only be able to speak *nihongo*. Should this attitude seem surprising, even unbelievable, many other attitudes equally strange will emerge in the course of this book.

When I returned to England in the winter of 1984, after two years' absence in Japan, I was surprised at the continuing lack of interest about Japan among most British people, despite the fact that Britain's economy is becoming more and more interlocked with Japan's, and that many people's houses – and garages – are stuffed with Japanese products. Even among those reasonably well informed about foreign affairs, there was an unusual ignorance and, more worrying, an indifference about Japan. This is in sharp contrast to the interest in the United States in Japan at every level, from culture to economics.

One evening I saw a television programme about Japanese life called *Sukiyaki and Chips*, a reference to Japan's favourite steak dish, and Japan's growing dominance in the international computer industry. It was a catchy enough title as an essentially English play on words, but wholly nonsensical in relation to Japan. But the absurdity of the title happily reflected the irrelevance of the programme. This scarcely related to real life in modern Japan but, in its own trivial way, helped to perpetuate that *Madame Butterfly* image which for too long has obscured the western view of Japan and the Japanese.

A large part of the programme, supposedly some kind of analysis of contemporary Japanese life, was devoted to gloating shots taken in an ultra-sophisticated and no doubt wildly expensive Tokyo strip club. The club's titillating speciality is to present strip shows using scenes from the famous plays of the traditional kabuki theatre. I happened to know the moving scene being used, one of the most famous in all kabuki. It was as tasteful as a London stripper playing out Ophelia's mad scene, and hardly more relevant to the life of modern Japan. There are certainly many strip clubs in Japan, most as seedy as those in Soho or Stockholm, but the one in the programme was wholly untypical. Programmes about even typical strip clubs, while they may be good for audience ratings, do little to explain the Japanese way of life to the rest of the world. Most Japanese never set foot inside a strip club.

The world is waking up slowly to the reality of Japan. I should add, in fairness, that Japan also remains blind to much of the real world around it, but that is more a matter of misunderstanding than indifference. For most western people, if they think of Japan at all, it remains a distant, exotic place of pagodas, geisha girls and cherry blossom, ideas which have lingered on from the west's first meeting with Japan in the nineteenth century. Older people's memories of the Second World War still cast a perplexing shadow across this picturesque landscape. The brutality of the Japanese military seems so horribly at odds with the gentleness and sensitivity apparent in so much of Japanese life.

The west's familiarity with and fondness for Japanese manu-factured goods, admired for their design, ingenuity and reli-ability, has added another dimension and complication to the western view of Japan, matched by a growing suspicion of Japan's workaholic success which is aggravating the severe trade friction with the United States and the EEC. Old and new images of Japan are becoming further confused and are producing a new conception of Japan which moves even further from the truth.

When I see television programmes such as the one I have described, and read more and more articles in the press which intentionally or unintentionally propagate a false idea of Japan, I feel both anger and sorrow. I can understand that the press must sell newspapers by icing the often stodgy cake of fact with exotic trivia. But in the case of Japan there is little need for fiction. There is so much in Japanese life that is genuinely exotic, bizarre, and at times almost unbelievable – and these are all an integral part of daily Japanese life.

I hope this book, while written as a personal view of Japan, will give the reader an accurate account of at least part of this fascin-ating country. The book is the story of a journey through Japan, roughly 2000 miles from the cold coastline of northern Hokkaido, down the main group of islands, and south across the Pacific to the white beaches of Okinawa. To be more exact, it is an amalgam of many journeys made throughout Japan during the past eight-een years. The journeys were made under many different cir-cumstances, with many different companions. While I hope the facts and figures are up to date, I have borrowed freely from past experiences and impressions where such memories still seemed relevant. Even when Japan changes, it changes slowly. By Japanese standards, eighteen years is but a small moment of time. But during those years the face of Japan has changed considerably. How far the heart and mind of Japan have changed during the same period is a major concern of this book, and a difficult question to answer.

I first arrived in Japan in September 1967. My impressions of my arrival and first evening in Tokyo remain vivid. I had come to Japan to mount a large historical exhibition about the Victorian period in Tokyo's largest department store. The big stores are the most active sponsors of art and other kinds of exhibitions, although in 1967 such large exhibitions were a novelty.

As I came out of the aircraft, at the foot of the steps was a reception committee complete with a large banner welcoming me to Japan. Exhaustion and this first wave of Japanese hospitality nearly overwhelmed me. I recall a tedious episode with a bureaucratic customs official. The Japanese had insisted on including a small wax statue of Queen Victoria, so fragile that I carried it with me in a special box. On hearing the name of the department store, this conscientious officer presumed that I was going to sell the statue. I was showered with import documents and a demand for the box to be opened. The special construction of the box would have made that difficult there and then. Fortunately, at the moment of total impasse, an official from the British embassy released me from the grip of Japanese petty bureaucracy.

I finally reached my hotel room in a state of some exhaustion and the sense of being surrounded by so many new experiences. My hosts owned a chain of splendid hotels, so I found myself in a beautiful room of an immaculate cleanliness I have never seen rivalled outside Japan. I stood watching the twilight darken southern Tokyo. Below, a variety of contrasting landmarks summarised in one narrow view many of the enigmas of modern Japan. The hotel stood in the shadow of the huge, skeletal Tokyo Tower, a post-war symbol of Japanese aspirations for western culture in all its manifestations. In a typically Japanese way, by adding some kind of aerial to the top of the main structure, the Japanese can now claim that the Tokyo Tower is the highest in the world.

To the right of the hotel, and far more impressive, spread the grey tiled roofs of the great Zojoji temple, Buddhist guardian of the southern section of the old city and only just inside the southern gateway of Edo, as Tokyo was called. To my left, across a modern avenue, glittered a crimson and gold building in the Chinese style. I learned later that this was an expensive Chinese restaurant. For the rest, the view was basically of a modern and monotonous townscape, raised expressways, riding over the roofs of smaller buildings and snaking between the higher office blocks. In the background was a huge green haze. This was not the trees of some small park but the surrounding netting of a large baseball ground.

That first evening was punctuated with small surprises. I noticed that even the most familiar things seemed to be slightly different. It was the beginning of what is called cultural shock, although in my case I found it a delicious sensation. The elegance of the hotel was impeccable, but there was a self-consciousness about the western-style restaurant which made it quite unlike any restaurant in Europe. The immaculate waiters had the air of people taking part in a difficult play while not absolutely sure of either their moves or their lines. The wine waiter served a pleasant but ordinary bottle of Japanese wine with the reverence due to a great vintage burgundy, basket and all. Even today, wherever the plonk is served, a cork hardly off the tree is solemnly presented for inspection.

Back in my room I found a cotton kimono and sash neatly folded by my pillow. In the bathroom was not only soap but also a neat kit containing a toothbrush, a tiny tube of toothpaste and a disposable razor. My own luggage began to seem superfluous, particularly as a one-hour express laundry service was offered. What puzzled me most was a vase of hideous plastic flowers perched on top of the lavatory cistern. It not only seemed out of place but was wholly at odds with all I knew about Japanese aesthetics, attitudes to nature and the subtle tradition of Japanese flower arrangement.

Each of these things was trivial in itself, but they were my first experience of Japan's bewildering difference and how the most familiar things take on a new and mysterious identity in Japan. In the light of eighteen years' experience such things have ceased to surprise me. I have learned that each seeming inconsistency fits logically, if often circuitously, into the pattern of Japanese life which is usually different rather than inscrutable.

While writing this book during the past year, I have been travelling widely again, visiting parts of Japan I had missed before, or returning to places which have particularly impressed me previously, either for their beauty or their special interest. Along the way, I have walked through many urban streets, some a quaint huddle of low wooden houses and quietness, elsewhere neighbourhoods scarred with the cheap glitter of commercial development. In the big cities the uncontrolled urban sprawl spreads wider. In the countryside, the small towns and villages fare little better. Within walking distance of my house two small mountains have been partly dismantled to provide new building sites. Nothing is sacred while more and more becomes profane. This has been the landscape of my years in Japan. It is a landscape peopled with Japanese friends, acquaintances, business associates and academic colleagues. This total experience has been my main study and is the raw material of this book, which I have tried to shape into a personal and an impressionistic but, I hope, balanced view of Japan.

Japan is a nation of four main islands and over 4000 smaller ones. The Japanese archipelago stretches in a curve close to the mainland of the Soviet Union, China and Korea. The Japan Sea lies to the west and the Pacific Ocean to the east. Japan's main islands lie roughly in the latitudes of central France to northern Algeria, or Oregon to lower California. The four main islands, from north to south, are Hokkaido, Honshu, Shikoku and Kyushu. A few largish islands lie around their coast, and 800 km to the south is the semi-tropical group of Okinawa.

The land area of Japan is about 370,000 sq km, approximately 25 per cent larger than the British Isles, or equal to West and East Germany combined, or the State of California. But the vital statistic in understanding Japan's economy, her social structure and many of her problems, is that some 75 per cent of the land surface is mountainous and largely uninhabitable. Nor can most of this area be cultivated. Mostly the mountains are small but they are too steep to terrace. They are mainly forested and fruit is grown on the lower slopes. This shortage of flat, inhabitable land has been a problem for centuries. Now, as Japan's population edges towards 120 million, the problem grows ever more acute. Prosperity has brought a vastly increased car ownership and stimulated demand for better houses and greater leisure and sports facilities, all of which are frustrated by lack of space. Space is now Japan's most precious commodity, a fact reflected in soaring land values.

Japan is now divided into forty-seven administrative areas. There are forty-three prefectures, the two urban areas of Osaka and Kyoto, the metropolitan area of Tokyo, and the district of Hokkaido island. Each of the areas has its own local government with elected representatives and considerable local power, though always dependent on central government for financial subsidy, particularly in the development of the poorer regions. The basic system is not dissimilar to the pattern of local government in Britain and the United States.

In describing Japan in this book, I have split the country into ten regions. There are a number of traditional or recognised ways of dividing up Japan. Rather than follow one particular system, I have made the division in the way that best fitted the pattern of this book. I hope it will prove the simplest to those unfamiliar with the geography of Japan. People tend to think of Japan as running roughly north to south, parallel with the mainland. This is not so and is a confusing idea. If you look at the map of Japan you will see that while the upper half of Japan runs roughly from north to south, about half-way down the island of Honshu, the lower half of Japan turns sharply to the west. The Japanese have long tended to think of western and eastern Japan and to make geographical descriptions in those terms. Kyoto was the western capital until Tokyo was made the eastern capital.

Usually the largest island, Honshu, is divided into five regions. Of these, for example, the six northern prefectures form the region called Tohoku, while the five southernmost prefectures make up the region of Chugoku. There are more complicated systems of division: one can speak of northern Honshu and western Honshu but never southern Honshu. For the reader's convenience I have created a hybrid system. For example, I have removed Tokyo and Kyoto from their districts of Kanto and Kansai since both demand separate treatment. I hope my system will be clear as the journey progresses, but readers will find reference to the maps helpful. The geography of Japan is complicated, and it is made more confusing by difficult and unfamiliar place names, many of which may appear confusingly similar.

One of my main purposes has been to show the relationship between the Japanese people and their natural environment, for in that relationship lie many of the clues to the character of the Japanese and their outlook on life. In one way this is a journey through the physical world of Japan, both town and countryside, from the beautiful and picturesque to the dull and ugly. But the main purpose of this journey is to observe Japanese life at different levels and from such observations to try and explain how this enigmatic country works.

The Industrial Revolution has separated people everywhere from their natural environment and from traditional, rural life. Japan, despite the fact that it is now the second largest industrial economy in the world, has, in certain ways, retained, amidst its massive urbanisation, traditional rural thinking and attitudes. These ties with the past may vanish, but at present the relationship with nature still has a deep influence on most Japanese. For the city dwellers, nature has become little more than an abstract idea, but it is an idea still at the heart of life.

The basic pattern of this book is simple. Each chapter is

devoted to one region, or one city. First there is a general description of that region, with some comment on a few places or things of particular interest or unique to that area. In the second part of each chapter I have used the dominant character of each region to exemplify certain elements of the Japanese character and Japanese life. I have not struggled for uniformity and the pattern is shaped to suit the subject-matter. I hope that by weaving the landscape and its people together, the resulting picture will reveal something of Japan and its people.

Japan is an exceptionally homogeneous country, racially and in its basic attitudes to life, spiritual and social. There are large foreign communities of Koreans and Chinese living in Japan, but although many of them have lived in Japan for more than one generation, they are deliberately segregated from Japanese society. In reality, Japanese blood is not as pure as most Japanese people like to think. This is obvious from the great variety of facial types found in Japan. However, the first lesson in understanding the Japanese is that their conception of life and themselves involves a number of myths. However absurd or even distasteful these may seem to the outsider, one must accept them as part of Japanese reality, believed in by all. Each culture nurses such myths. In Japan they tend to be more potent than in other industrialised societies.

This close-knit sense of identity gives a certain uniformity to the whole of Japanese society. There are regional differences. But it would be misleading to over-emphasise them. Equally, it would be a distortion to apply sweeping generalisations to the whole of Japan. Much is basically the same everywhere, but everywhere there are differences. Modern life is bringing many changes and breaking up old regional patterns.

Most foreign visitors would travel the length of Japan without being aware of any changes between the different regions, except to note that some were more rural and poorer than others. They would probably miss the changes in accent and dialect, the variety of local foods and other products, differences in domestic architecture and other indications of local traditional life. At a deeper level, traits of character rooted in local conditions, such as the rugged independence of the northerners, the extreme reserve of Kyoto people or the openness of Osaka people would be missed. Even after years of daily contact, such things are never obvious. In Japan first impressions are so often misleading. More than in most countries, things are seldom what they appear to be. This makes Japan the more fascinating; it also makes it the more perplexing.

Most of the ten areas of Japan suggest one or more elements in the Japanese character or Japanese society which can be better understood and discussed against the background of that area. Tokyo prompts the question: how westernised is post-war Japan? The old capital of Kyoto conjures up all that is most traditional in Japanese life and prompts the opposite question: how can so much tradition survive in such a technological society? But although these themes are discussed in the context of a particular city or region, they are in no sense regional, and to some degree are common to all of Japan.

One fact about this book may suggest an omission to the reader who does not know Japan. Where are the crowds that overwhelm the traveller in India and other eastern countries? One might expect to be crushed at every turn by Japan's enormous population living in such a comparatively small area. It is true that crowds are easily found at the weekends in the main shopping areas or on the urban transport systems during the morning and evening rush hours. But even in those densely crowded situations the masses of people are so disciplined and self-effacing, they do not have the impact of the hordes of India and China. And while the Japanese continually complain of overcrowding, some of it is of their own making. If you prefer to go with the crowd, inevitably you immediately form one. The descriptions and photographs in this book are not depopulated by some trick or by any special effort. It remains surprisingly easy to get away from it all. From where I now live in Kyoto, three minutes down the hill by bicycle and I am in a busy shopping street faced with every urban convenience. Four minutes up the hill on foot and I am on forested mountain paths which lead for miles and where I seldom meet anyone. I suspect, and pray it may remain that way, that my 'neck of the woods' has not yet been recommended in the official Japanese guide-books. Fortunately, the Japanese do not care to wander off the approved track.

The subject is too huge for one short book. All that I have written is highly selective. The journey through Japan is not a conventional or comprehensive guide-book. I have selected a few places in each region which are particularly interesting, characteristic of that area, or simply places I have enjoyed for one reason or another. However, I think I can say that if a visitor followed my itinerary, they would have an unusual but rewarding time in Japan. The Japanese character is infinitely larger than the islands which contain this distinctive people. Here I have tried to touch on what I feel to be most important while painfully aware of my many omissions.

East Meets West

TOKYO

I could describe Tokyo in terms of statistics, enumerating its skyscrapers or its museums, or by delineating it in terms of the dozens of railway lines which are the veins and arteries of this sprawling metropolis. All that can come later. I prefer to start with more intimate, small-scale memories. For me the charm and pleasures of Tokyo must be winkled out of back streets and obscure corners which hide behind the dull façades of the great avenues, the public buildings, the towering hotels and all the other paraphernalia of a huge modern city.

It was hot and sticky that September evening. A group of mature Japanese students I had recently looked after in England were welcoming me to Tokyo with a dinner party. When I met their own teachers at their school, it was too early to go to the restaurant and taking a train to Ueno in the northern part of the city, we passed the time wandering around that part of Tokyo. A slight breeze ruffled heavy lotus nodding over the waters of the famous Shinobazu pond. It was too late for the spectacular display of deep blue flowers, but the wide lake, with its walkways and the picturesque Bentendo temple, exotically enshrining an Indian goddess of good fortune, held us seemingly in a quiet and private world. It seemed far from the hot sidewalks and the commuter crush of Tokyo which in fact lay just beyond the line of trees. Oases can be found within the frenzy of Tokyo where one may fleetingly enjoy the illusion of an older world.

The restaurant also had a pleasant rural air. The students had booked a large upstairs room. The open windows looked down onto a courtyard garden. In one corner an old camellia tree spread its shade and somewhere from its roots a stream sparkled between rocks and ferns, running into a small pond where gold, white, crimson and silver carp nosed against the trickling water. The evening was full of food, laughter, the crisp taste of ice-cold Kirin beer and a gentle sense of belonging that is often generated by a Japanese group.

Like an overgrown carp myself, I sat by the window gasping in every breath of air. It was strange to mingle our reminiscences of West Sussex with the sights and sounds of this obscure corner of Tokyo. The maids bustled in and out, hot-cheeked in their dark blue kimonos and bright yellow sashes. More and more trays of food, more bottles of beer, until the low tables were stacked only with empty dishes. It was hard to believe that only one month before I had sat in a teashop a stone's throw from the Brighton Pavilion eating cheap cream buns with this same group of Japanese, sheltering from a cold rain that lashed the sea-front. As always, it was good to be back in Tokyo.

Tokyo has a fascinating history and a distinctive character but there are times when the city seems to defy you to find them. The erosions of time, the terrible earthquake and resultant fires of 1923, and the fire-bombs of the Second World War have destroyed most of the physical past of the city. It was founded with the name of Edo by the Tokugawa shoguns in 1603, their new 'political capital'. It did not become the official capital of Japan, when its name was changed to Tokyo, until 1868 when the Emperor Meiji moved from the old capital of Kyoto. Only fragments are left of nearly 400 years of history, scattered across this vast modern urban landscape which has an elusive character of its own. But at every turning and at each street corner, the meeting of east and west is obvious in this city of 11 million people.

For the casual visitor to Japan, Tokyo is often their only disappointment. One is likely to be disappointed if you expect from Tokyo the qualities and atmosphere you find in London, Paris or New York. The charms of Tokyo are not obvious. They require time to search out and enjoy. With the obvious exception of things Japanese, such as great Japanese restaurants and the magnificent public and private collections of Japanese art, many other things in Tokyo tend to be secondhand and better done elsewhere. I find the public face of Tokyo mostly unattractive and each year more horribly commercialised. Recently a famous Paris restaurant opened a branch in Tokyo, and it was advertised as 'the most expensive restaurant in the world'; what an extraordinary form of recommendation. Tokyo is the ultimate consumer city, itself producing little significant modern art, intellectual or literary life and no great modern theatre; and with a social scene that is exceptionally provincial. Budapest was more stimulating even in its darkest years.

It is difficult to master Tokyo's sprawling geography, to fix in one's mind a simple map of even the central area of this amorphous city. It has no easily remembered basic plan and few distinctive monuments. Like many other big cities, it is an agglomeration of separate districts which have merged into each other, their individuality destroyed largely by flood and fire and the grey hand of commercial development. Despite the long time I have spent in Tokyo, as I move through the city by bus or taxi, I am often uncertain through which anonymous neighbourhood I am passing.

In practice the problem of getting about Tokyo is solved largely by its excellent and huge subway system, linked to a number of suburban lines. This is the only certain way to arrive on time anywhere since the centre of Tokyo now lives with a round-the-clock traffic jam. The subway system is simple to use except at some of the main stations where several lines converge. These are vast beyond belief and fairly confusing. But those who keep their heads usually arrive safely at their destinations.

Gruesome stories of the Tokyo rush hour and the 'crowd pushers' squeezing the commuters into the carriages have gone around the world. I think they are rather exaggerated. I would not advise anyone to catch a train at Piccadilly Circus around five-thirty in the afternoon, and not infrequently I have seen a London Transport official give a hefty shove to get the doors closed. I have been a commuter in both London and Tokyo. By and large both were exhausting experiences, but at least in Tokyo during the hot weather the trains are air-conditioned. In recent years female travellers on the Tokyo subway have complained more loudly about the prevalence of bottom-pinchers. Whether this un-welcome practice is part of the process of westernisation or simply human nature I am not qualified to judge.

For most people the centre of Tokyo is the Ginza (Plate 2). Although the Ginza clusters around one great shopping avenue, it is not a single street but a district, named after the silver mint once in the area. Today it is devoted to shopping, restaurants and entertainment with a small and expensive nightclub area. The Ginza leads two lives. There is the glitter of the main streets, all great department stores and smart specialist shops. Behind, in a maze of narrow backstreets, lined with smaller shops, bars and restaurants, delivery vans, scooters and pedestrians battle for the right to life. I enjoy the Ginza and its life and commerce always offer an hour or two of free entertainment.

Whatever Tokyo may lack in artistic and intellectual life, it probably has the most exciting shopping in the world. This ranges from the intriguing variety of traditional Japanese objects to an unrivalled range of goods from around the world, at equally unrivalled high prices. At the centre of all this are the leading department stores, a major feature of Japanese life, with branches all over Japan. For the Japanese shopping is not simply a matter of buying things you want. It is a way of life, a major form of entertainment. The big stores respond to this in many ways and are both shopping centres and places of entertainment. They offer an enormous range of Japanese and foreign goods. They also offer a range of services that would sustain you from the cradle to the grave, with special provision for present-giving which is such an important part of Japanese life. And to tempt you further there are large art exhibitions from Europe, exhibitions by well-known Japanese artists, and displays of wares for the tea-ceremony and examples of flower-arrangement.

Ordinary neighbourhood shopping is extremely good in the larger towns and I have often asked friends why they bother to go to the big stores. The answer is always the same. The stores offer extra variety and, more important, it is an enjoyable way to spend an afternoon. I must say that whenever I go to a store – and I also find them entertaining – I see many people looking but seemingly few buying. In Japan window shopping is done from the inside. Despite that I know that a big store in Tokyo can easily turn over 280 million yen (£1 million) over a weekend. They are all fully open on both Saturday and Sunday, the time for big spending.

In the centre of the Ginza is one of the two Tokyo branches of Tokyo's oldest department store: Mitsukoshi, first established in Edo in 1673 as a dry goods store. Mitsukoshi Ginza is typical of many large stores, nearly all of which are laid out in the same way. Thus the customers know that they will find handkerchiefs on the first floor, kimonos on the third floor and a variety of restaurants on the sixth or seventh floor, or both. Nothing is more overwhelming than the food basement, in large stores two basements. These provide a breathtaking visual encyclopedia of world food and drink. But the star attraction is always the Japanese section, not only for the range of exotic foods but for the exquisite or ingenious wrappings, be it tea folded in elegant green paper with a pattern of pine trees dusted in gold, or a lump of fermented vegetable wrapped with nautical neatness in rice straw.

It was my association with Seibu Department Stores, one of the largest and most enterprising groups, that first brought me to Japan in 1967, and brought me back several times in the following years. Some of this story is worth telling since many events illustrate Japanese commercial life. Also my first visit ended with an unexpected and unusual privilege. Seibu opened many doors and gave me many insights and experiences, not least the opportunity to work for a major Japanese company, with a kind and most tolerant group of colleagues.

In 1967 Seibu, though rapidly on the way up, were polishing their image which, in relation to Mitsukoshi, was roughly Selfridges to Harrods or Maceys to Saks. Their main Tokyo store, in the suburb of Ikebukuro, was already the biggest in Japan and they were intent on prestige promotion. Seibu were pioneers in presenting major art and historical exhibitions in department stores.

Through the British Board of Trade, for these exhibitions usually went hand in hand with trade fairs, Seibu achieved a coup in getting permission to bring Queen Victoria's coronation robes from the then London Museum in Kensington Palace to Tokyo. They had never left England before. It was decided to frame this royal centrepiece in an exhibition of Victorian paintings and objects together with a collection of other royal personalia. Since most of the Victorian art was borrowed from the Birmingham Museum & Art Gallery, of which I was then Director, I was invited to supervise the exhibition and to accompany it to Tokyo, together with the senior restorer from the London Museum.

The whole experience was new to Seibu. They had pulled out all the stops in Tokyo and when I arrived the exhibits had been safely stored in the vaults of the National Museum. Time was short. The exhibition was to open at 9 a.m. three days after my arrival. This tight schedule had already alarmed me. I became more alarmed on my first morning when my new colleagues seemed unwilling to show me the exhibition area at Ikebukuro. We had a brief meeting, a glance at the crates in stores, and I was taken sightseeing.

Even in the large London museums it took four or five weeks to mount a major exhibition. This Victorian exhibition contained at least 300 objects, requiring glass cases and special display. At lunch on the second day, as we sat idly in a beautiful Japanese restaurant, eating delicious steaks and looking out over an exquisite garden, none of these delights calmed or comforted me. Almost in tears, I begged my hosts to put me out of my misery, to tell me what was planned, and to explain how we were about to achieve the impossible.

They weakened. We returned to Ikebukuro and went up to the men's clothing floor. We walked through a forest of suits and overcoats and gazed down a long vista of shirts and socks. Yes, this was the exhibition area. The second the store closed on the eve of the exhibition, the area would be cleared and the exhibition mounted overnight. The sheer impossibility of the whole thing became greater than ever. A nervous fear was replaced by terror.

My Japanese colleagues were wholly unperturbed. It would be uneconomic to remove the shirts and socks any earlier. Everything was under control. I prayed, but without much faith in a positive response.

On the last day the action started. I soon realised that while the Japanese have their own methods, nothing is left to chance. A long meeting of the exhibition team revealed the plan of campaign. Everything had been thought out down to the last fold in Queen Victoria's coronation robes. I learned two interesting facts. First, at six o'clock sharp, an army of carpenters and electricians would move in to transform the shirt and sock department. In Japan space is often more costly than labour. Second, we would work all night with a break at eight to freshen up for the official opening at nine. Nobody apologised. Working all night was simply part of the job. At last I saw the point of the socialising and sightseeing with the Japanese team since my arrival. This strange Englishman must be assimilated into their existing group so that when the work started, he would function properly as a member of the group. What is more, this swift piece of structuring had worked. My identity was now as part of that admirable team.

I shall always remember two things, two Japanese lessons, about that night. Throughout the night, a gentle good humour took the friction out of everyone's exhaustion. Japanese humour is not particularly subtle, but the Japanese like to laugh. Laughter and good humour are essential lubricants in their pressured lives. Second, though we were working frantically against the clock, every object in the exhibition was handled with a care near to reverence I have never seen equalled: each man who handled the objects wore spotless white gloves which were immediately changed for new ones when slightly dirty. This seemed an outward sign of the inner seriousness with which everyone took their work. It was a memorable experience to work in such a dedicated team.

After the opening of the exhibition, not having been to Japan before, I had hoped to sneak off for a few days' sightseeing. I had brought the necessary money and a list of the places I most wanted to see, a long list. At lunch the Seibu representative looking after me told me that it was not necessary for me to stay in Tokyo during the exhibition. Seibu would like to give me a sightseeing holiday around Japan until it was time to return and pack up the exhibition. Embarrassed by their hospitality, I assured my friend that I already had everything organised. Never try to refuse Japanese hospitality. Within ten minutes my travels were in the hands of Mr Tanaka, and so was my long list of places which he insisted on borrowing.

Twenty-four hours later a bulging envelope of tickets, money, hotel vouchers and itinerary were put into my hands, and a few hours after that I set off on a magic carpet tour of Japan with a delightful guide. I remain puzzled how they did it. With exact planning and use of aircraft, cars and boats and the 'bullet train', I was taken to every place on my extremely comprehensive list. That was my first journey 'Into Japan.'

It was the last night of our tour and we were sitting in the International Hotel at Toba discussing, of all things, Shakespeare's sonnets. At 9 p.m. my telephone rang: it was the president of Seibu Department Stores, sounding rather nervous.

'Lowe-san, I have a great favour to ask of you. I hope very much you will be able to help us.'

'Of course, I will do anything I can, Mori-san.'

'Lowe-san,' a long indrawing of breath came anxiously down the line. 'Lowe-san, the Emperor of Japan has asked if it would be possible to move the exhibition to the Imperial Palace so that he and the Empress may have a private view. I must explain that the Emperor was willing to visit the exhibition at Ikebukuro, but the Tokyo police thought it unwise in view of the vast crowds.' An even longer breath . . . a beseeching pause. 'I hope you can help us. It would have to be tomorrow night.'

We caught the milk train from Toba to Tokyo and there began one of the most hectic twenty-four hours of my life. We could do little until 6 p.m. when the exhibition finally closed. That night often comes back to me in a series of vivid scenes, more like shots from a Hollywood movie than private memories. The workmen returned, moving around the exhibition like an army of ants. Slowly, agonisingly slowly, the crates were filled as our watches moved on. Yet, by midnight everything was safely stowed into immaculate steel vans with padded interiors. The procession formed.

Nothing had been spared. When Japan's largest private company combines with the Imperial Household, things happen. At the centre of this midnight entourage were seven steel vans. At the front and back were a number of limousines with the necessary personnel. But it was the formidable police escort that gave the occasion a special drama. Just after midnight we pulled away from Ikebukuro. With sirens at full howl, the leading police cars and their motorcycle outriders accelerated to the kind of speed only allowed to city police. We screamed down the centre of the road, ignoring lights, the odd cruising car or taxi waved to the kerbside, straight through to the centre of Tokyo and one of the main gates into the Imperial Palace and to the concert hall where we were to display the exhibition. Somehow the objects were displayed in a reasonable way and by 7.30 a.m. I was miraculously back in my hotel room for a quick bath and a change of shirt. Even so, time was short. I had promised to get myself back to the Imperial Palace by 8.40 a.m. Feeling tidy but tired and nervous, I asked the head porter to get me a taxi to the Imperial Palace. He looked at me strangely and I repeated my request. He looked embarrassed. Was it my English or my request that he did not understand? I don't suppose it was something he was asked for every day. At last I persuaded him that I was a genuine caller at that august address and after he had given the driver the name of the particular gate, once again I was on my way.

By 8.55 a.m. the small group to be presented to the Emperor and Empress were lined up in the lobby of the concert hall. My colleagues had warned me that the palace chamberlains were often rather officious. As we were waiting, one elderly gentleman approached me and with a stern look advised me that His Imperial Majesty did not shake hands. To be honest I had not expected that he would. When approached I should give an extremely low bow. This seemed straightforward enough. At exactly nine o'clock, a large car drew up at the steps leading to the concert hall. The Emperor and Empress had arrived. The Emperor moved swiftly down the line, but not wishing to appear curious, I stared straight ahead. Suddenly, the Emperor was three feet in front of me. An official gave my name and I started to go into an extremely low bow. To my dismay, just as I had got low enough to be slightly off balance, I saw the Emperor moving briskly towards me – *under* me would be more accurate – to shake hands. I managed to stop, my nose some four inches above collision point. I had been badly advised.

After that false start, the whole occasion was delightful and extremely informal. The Emperor's great interest in everything and the warmth of the Empress made all the effort worthwhile. Often such royal occasions are rather perfunctory, but the Emperor examined every object, asked many informed questions and the inspection lasted about two hours. Although the Emperor spoke through an interpreter, it was obvious from his reactions that he was frequently ahead. I remember he was much amused by the confusion Queen Victoria had caused the customs official. On one or two occasions he assisted the interpreter. We were examining the flowers of the Commonwealth countries on the coronation robes of our present Queen, but the poor interpreter was defeated when we came to Australia. The Emperor leant forward and peered at the gold embroidery.

'Ah so, mimosa,' he murmured.

But he is well known for his botanical knowledge. His knowledge of the British royal family was also considerable. Perhaps his main reason for wishing to see this exhibition was his nostalgia for that short and happy stay he had had in Britain as a young man which he has never forgotten, particularly the kindness of Edward VII.

It was an extraordinary experience. I often think that the Emperor of Japan, that small, quiet, scholarly but impressive man, must have led almost the strangest life of anyone alive. Born a god, he was destined, over the radio, to deny his divinity to his shattered countrymen. I have certainly never enjoyed more showing anyone around an exhibition. Expert in his own field of marine biology the Emperor had a sharp eye, wide interests and he made it an easy occasion for all of us by his quiet humour and charm. Behind it all lay serene strength which he must often have needed during his troubled reign, now the longest in Japanese history.

The Imperial Palace occupies a large area in the centre of Tokyo. It was taken over from the Tokugawas by Emperor Meiji. At first a castle, its origins can still be seen in the wide moat, stone walls and handsome gateways, white walls and heavy wooden gates topped by grey-tiled roofs (Plate 11). The palace is an attractive centrepiece for the city, if not a great help to its traffic problems. Inside, a variety of smallish buildings are scattered about the grounds, mostly of recent date. The Emperor is said to prefer a simple way of life, ever impatient to escape to his laboratory.

The area of Tokyo around the Imperial Palace has long been known as the 'high city', the healthier and wealthier district where in Edo times the Shogun's followers and the visiting provincial lords had their houses. To the north-east lay the 'low city', the poorer but more colourful area. Here the puritanical Edo government tried to isolate all popular forms of entertainment including the theatre. On the far outskirts was Yoshiwara, the famous licensed brothel quarter and the home of what has come to be known as the 'floating world'. Time has obliterated much of the difference between these areas as land values soar throughout the metropolitan area, and the ordinary office worker commutes three or four hours a day to the outer suburbs. Some traces of the past linger in the 'low city' district of Asakusa, which is not to be confused with the gilded cabaret-land of central Akasaka.

Asakusa is still one of the cheap entertainment districts of Tokyo, with many small restaurants and bars and a few popular theatres. To the stranger it is mostly faceless streets but a lot of raw life exists there. The heart is the Sensoji or the Asakusa

Kannon temple, of no real architectural merit but full of atmosphere. From the main street a massive wooden gateway leads
under a huge paper lantern to a lane flanked with small shops,
leading to the temple. The shops are bright with cheap trinkets
and souvenirs. In spring the lane is decked out with plastic cherry
blossom while plastic wistaria and maple leaves announce summer and autumn. It is a busy place as the crowd moves among the
shops and pushes towards the temple. A large courtyard fronts the
temple steps. In the middle is a bronze incense-burner. The
Japanese crowd round the great bowl, their hands drawing the
sweet smoke to painful parts of their body, believing that it will
effect a cure.

The drift of incense reminds me of my favourite Tokyo pilgrimage, to one of those quiet corners where against all the odds
history has survived. To the south-east, in the area of Takanawa,
near Tokyo port, is the small, concealed temple of Sengakuji,
burial place of Japan's most famous and popular heroes, the
Forty-Seven Ronin. In 1701 the Lord Asano, while visiting Edo,
was provoked into drawing his sword against the Lord Kira.
Asano was ordered to commit suicide. His forty-seven loyal
retainers swore revenge. Waiting patiently for several months, to
put Kira off his guard, in the snow of December 1702 they
surrounded Kira's house and killed him. They calmly announced
their deed to the authorities, and obeying the official and inevitable judgement, all committed suicide near this small temple
where the Lord Asano had been buried.

This heroic story has been a major subject for the Japanese
theatre, and more recently for a number of fine films. It epitomises all that the Japanese admire in the quality of loyalty and its
most extreme obligations, a vital element in Japanese feudal
society.

In a simple, melancholy graveyard by the temple, in order of
seniority the Forty-Seven Ronin's graves surround the burial
place of their lord. The stones are humble markers but there are
always offerings and flowers, and a haze of incense drifts across
the burial ground. It is a moving place. Within the temple they

keep the address made by the ronin's leader to his dead lord just before taking his own life. It is said that no one can read those words without being moved to tears. Perhaps simply the atmosphere of this quiet place is poignant enough. It is such places as this that make Tokyo memorable – where moments of history reach out from among the skyscrapers and the pleasure palaces, reviving the past and giving thought for the future.

Modern Tokyo has some spectacular sights and extraordinary contrasts, a world neatly summed up by the shop assistant who ignores her computerised cash-till to make lightning calculations with her Japanese abacus. There is the new Disneyland, third in the world; a number of towering hotels whose breathtaking architecture (Plate 22) and modern facilities are matched by their perfect service. Of the traditional world there are Japanese restaurants with private rooms as elegant as the geisha who entertain there. Hardly less exotic, if more up to date, are the weird cult-groups of young dancers of Harajuku, while no one should miss the equally colourful autumn chrysanthemum shows. And no visit to Tokyo would be complete without a visit to Japan's traditional kabuki theatre, one of the most beautiful dramatic forms in the world in which simple stories and a stylised form of acting partly overcome the problem of not understanding the words. The performances last all day but one may come and go as one pleases. The first time I went I intended to stay an hour and stayed for five.

Roppongi is for the entertainment of the gilded youth of Tokyo, complete with smart discos and 'genuine' English pubs. The less wealthy young people flock to Shinjuku, Tokyo's most frenetic district, signposted in the sky by a Martian cluster of skyscrapers, where they gaze up at the vast video screen on the wall opposite the station swaying to the throb of a Stones' concert. All around there is a frenzied maze of restaurants, bars, *pachinko* pin-ball parlours, shrieking video-games halls, movie houses and love hotels, all screaming with life and, tragically, occasionally with death. Some of the young come to play, a few to disappear.

I find it hard to write other than impressionistically about

Tokyo. I have spent a lot of time there, but my experiences, my work, my sense of geography, even my memories remain fragmentary. It is that kind of city. There are also memories of people. Many of these friendships are also fleeting as, sadly, Japanese tend to drop one when one ceases to be a member of their group and the formal social relationship dissolves. I had many marvellous times with my Seibu colleagues who indulged my taste for raw fish and took me to restaurants of memorable luxury and elegance, the most magnificent run by a celebrated old lady who became the heroine of one of Yukio Mishima's most famous novels, *After the Banquet*. Each time I went there she showed me a menu card on which the English poet, Edmund Blunden, had written a brief poem for her. I was in Tokyo the afternoon of 25 November 1970 when Yukio Mishima ritually disembowelled himself and an extraordinary silence fell over Tokyo as the papers rushed out a special one-page edition.

For night life, there is all and more. My own experience is limited, but I did have one experience which was slightly amusing but mostly tragic. When I was working in Tokyo, I was often on my own and in the evenings I used to go to one of the enormous cabarets in Akasaka where there were over 500 hostesses and a brassy dance band. The system was civilised. A girl would come to your table but sat and talked for several minutes without accepting a drink. If you found her pleasant company you then offered her a drink. But if she found you unsympathetic, she would refuse, make an excuse to leave and shortly her place would be taken by another girl.

I got to know a striking-looking Korean girl and went and danced with her for three or four nights. Strictly speaking the girls are not supposed to date the customers and are well protected from unwelcome advances. Some of the girls there were readily 'available', some were respectable university students earning pocket money. All the girls use a pseudonym at the cabaret. On the fifth night the Korean girl came out to dinner with me. The cabaret closed at eleven and I was given strict instructions to wait for her in a coffee shop two streets away. We became friends and now I would meet her after her work when we had dinner and went to a disco. It was here that I learned the terrible truth. The disco was extremely dark. We sat up at the bar and after she had three times stubbed out her cigarette into someone else's whisky and then nearly fallen down the stairs, I realised that she was almost blind in semi-darkness.

She told me that she had an incurable eye disease and produced the thickest pair of spectacles I have ever seen. Her father had had the same disease and had gone blind very young. She was certain to do the same within the next few years. Like many Koreans in Japan she had had a hard life but even in the world of the cabaret she kept her integrity. When I returned to Tokyo about eight months later I went to the cabaret and asked my waiter for her, giving her pseudonym. To my dismay a completely different girl appeared. Evidently my girl had left and this newcomer had taken over her name. I made inquiries and telephoned her number, but she had vanished. I cannot be optimistic about what may have happened to her but I shall never know.

Tokyo and other large Japanese cities, which now house some 85 per cent of the population, present the visitor with a seemingly westernised face, and a largely matching western life-style. Wood gives place to concrete and plastic. Flat asphalt roofs replace the rippling sea of grey tiles. Where the doors still slide, they are of glass, not paper, and electronically operated. The commuter crowds – men in neat business suits, women in the latest European and American fashions – ride the most efficient, clean and punctual rail service in the world. Everywhere the shops are stocked with foreign goods and foreign food. Even the advertisements are headlined in English and often feature foreign models. In the face of this overwhelming evidence, it might seem unnecessary, even absurd, to ask, 'How westernised is Japan?'

Whether necessary or not, it is the question I am most often asked by visitors. True, they usually ask expecting the answer, 'Entirely', and are surprised when I reply, 'Hardly at all'. However, the fact that the question is asked so frequently does imply a lurking suspicion that behind the western appearances something different is going on.

I live in a traditional Japanese house and live partly in the Japanese style. I sleep on the floor, eat Japanese food and, sometimes in the house, wear Japanese clothes. But nobody ever asks me, 'How Japanised are you?' I have adopted this limited Japanese life-style because I like it, it is cheaper and more convenient here, and because the novelty of it all gives me some innocent fun. I think that many Japanese have exactly the same attitudes to their adoption of western ways into their habits. But those western objects and practices have little influence on their basic character, just as my cotton kimono does not change my English identity or attitudes to any significant extent.

I can carry this trifling comparison one step further. In certain cases I prefer Japanese domestic objects or practices because I think they are superior to their western counterparts. For the rest of my life I shall always, when possible, sleep in traditional Japanese bedding on the floor, unlike many Japanese who now spread their futon on a western bed. I do this simply because I think it is the most comfortable form of bedding in the world. I can also recommend it to fellow-sufferers of so-called 'slipped disc' back troubles.

From the beginning of the Meiji period, when Japan hurled herself into the Industrial Revolution, having remained so late a feudal and rural society, there has been an underlying feeling that western things are in some way superior, and maybe some things were for a long time. Japan was anxious to prove her modernity to the rest of the world. The attitude became ingrained and, sadly, many excellent Japanese objects and practices have been discarded for inferior western ways and means.

In all the arguments about the extent of Japanese westernisation, there is the lurking implication that 'western' and 'civilised' are synonymous, and that the western world is the source of all that is best. If you believe that, and many people do, then I suppose it is rude to question the westernisation of Japan. It makes it difficult to discuss the subject politely or rationally. I find this attitude provincial, if not outright arrogant, an echo of the old Christian missionary whose ideas now seem so absurdly out of date.

The Japanese have an old and distinctive civilisation which attained extraordinary sophistication when Europe was still submerged in the Dark Ages. Beyond that, China's civilisation, the inspiration of so much of Japan's culture, was, with Greece, one of two fountainheads of world civilisation. The Chinese achieved all of this without any help or borrowings from the west. In many respects it is wise, and suitably humbling, to ask if the west has been a source of inspiration or infection. Certainly the benevolence of western influence should never be taken for granted.

The Japanese are partly to blame for this attitude by their headlong rejection of the better things in their own cultural traditions for the sake of appearing modern. This was the fundamental debate of the Meiji period when almost every day, in the most practical ways, the Japanese authorities had to make far-reaching choices between 'east' and 'west'. At that time many Japanese leaders were overawed by the west, but a number of politicians, writers and intellectuals urged Japan 'to hasten slowly', taking from the west and the Industrial Revolution only those things suited to the needs of Japan, and particularly those that would blend with Japanese traditions.

Ogai Mori, the great Meiji novelist, who spent three years studying medicine in Germany in the late nineteenth century, fought all his life for a balanced marriage between Japanese tradition and new western knowledge. He epitomised his ideal in his own prose style which brilliantly combined Chinese rhetoric with a simple directness taken from European writers. This gave Mori a perfect means of expression for his deeply Japanese subjects.

So I would like to suggest that there is no 'inevitable' superiority about the western world. If this statement leaves you in doubt, compare your own country with Japan's low crime-rate, the almost 100 per cent rate of literacy, the small number of lawyers in Japan, the safety of the streets, the general lack of poverty, the success of Japanese industry. In the more traditional areas one must admire the greatness of the kabuki theatre, the continuing genius of textile design, the unrivalled skill of Japanese horticulture and the magic of their gardens. Far from being rude, should we discover that the westernisation of Japan is only superficial this could turn out to be a considerable compliment.

Nobody would deny that the Japanese have borrowed a great number of things from the west in the last century or so, from objects to etiquette. That is indisputable, and the borrowing has been on such a considerable scale that one might feel safe in presuming that traditional life has been largely swamped. Centuries ago, however, just as big a borrowing was made from China – far greater really, when one remembers that Buddhism became one of the main pillars of Japanese life and culture, while the west has basically failed to implant Christianity in Japan. Despite the massive borrowing from China, so universal that it is said that the folding fan is Japan's only wholly original contribution to traditional crafts, within a century or two the Japanese had comfortably digested everything and produced a new culture uniquely Japanese.

The question, therefore, is not how much Japan has borrowed from the west, but what have the Japanese done with those borrowings? Is that digestive process of the sixth and seventh centuries AD being repeated in the twentieth century, with the raw materials of western culture? That is certainly what I believe, putting an enormous process into an exceedingly small nutshell. At the most superficial level, western things cease to be wholly western once in Japan. Much deeper, behind any western façades, an extraordinary amount of traditional Japan remains intact; particularly all those things of real importance to the Japanese involving their national identity.

The almost universal use of western clothes appears a clinching argument for Japan's westernisation. But examining the ways in which Japanese men and women wear western clothes, I could list at least twenty-five ways in which western clothes become 'Japanised'. The most important area is the 'soft styling' of all clothes except the conventional business suit. There is also a marked unisex style in casual clothes that would be unthinkable in other countries, which suggests interesting facts about Japanese sexual identity. Even men dressed in the most formal business clothes seem to hark back to the comfort of the open-collared kimono, in that they seldom pull the knot of their tie tight to the neck. Every Japanese man is antipathetic to the western shoe with its enclosing hard back. Students tread down the backs of their sneakers to convert them into slippers, and businessmen discard them altogether when the occasion allows, openly in the train or furtively, one at a time, under the coffee shop table.

For fascinating cultural reasons, girls up to marriage frequently wear little-girl-style clothes – frilly blouses and lacy socks complete with ankle pom-poms – which a teenager would ridicule in Europe or the United States. The overcoat has not been accepted as proper formal wear. I watched a group of Japanese businessmen in freezing winter see their boss off on the train at Kyoto station. The chairman climbed aboard and stood snugly at the window while his juniors removed their overcoats to make their formal bows of farewell. The handkerchief is universal in Japan but only for a discreet mopping of the brow. In Japan it is polite to sniff but unthinkable to blow one's nose. How well I learned that fact. Five minutes after facing my first university class of some 120 nicely brought up girl students, unthinkingly I drew my handkerchief from my pocket and gave one of those uniquely British imitations of an elephant trumpeting; a hallmark of the British pedagogue, particularly if the handkerchief is grubby. At that moment I learned the true meaning of 'stunned silence'.

To look at it another way, the nature of the Japanese and the pattern of their lives ensures that in borrowing western clothes, adjustments of various kinds are inevitable. To some extent these change them into Japanese clothes. Nearly all Japanese people on occasions wear their traditional dress, which helps to keep traditional attitudes alive. The Japanese figure, male and female, is still considerably different from the western figure. Shoes are never worn indoors. The Japanese have an acute sense of season which profoundly affects attitude to dress, both style and quantity. Women have a 'soft' image, so even in the most outrageous punk fashion that image is preserved. The Japanese have a splendid obsession with personal cleanliness which leads to special influences and a complicated ritual concerning one's underclothes. These must never be left exposed when changing in a public place such as a bath-house. Long johns are still popular with older men, in winter for warmth, in summer partly to give continued protection from a dirty world. There are men's underpants which in fact are overpants to hide the tainted pants underneath; the upper pair have no front slit so that in summer trousers can be discarded with decency, something quite often done by men in trains.

I am too reticent to delve into the mysteries and idiosyncrasies of Japanese ladies' underwear, but the Japanese figure makes its own demands. Padded bras are the order of the day and a kind of samurai armour is donned in winter to keep out the cold, garments that would not have been out of place in the wardrobes of Victorian heroines. Pregnancy and the monthly period are dealt with in uniquely Japanese ways. Yet women are moving with the times: only recently a well-known fashion writer launched a scathing attack on the leading Japanese manufacturer of women's underclothes, accusing their designers of ignoring the changing line of the Japanese lady who is now in need of more support.

Taking such an everyday subject as clothing shows, I hope, that not even the most mundane things in Japanese life can be taken for granted as pure western imports. In seemingly obvious western goods one finds many modifications, not only in the object itself but in the Japanese attitude to it. Walking down any street the modern buildings are different, both the design and the materials; the food in the Italian restaurant is no more than an echo of real Italian food, while in the French restaurant opposite, the portions are so minute one seriously wonders why they bothered to dirty the glasses or the dishes. In the electrical shop, everything looks familiar enough. But that washing machine is far

1 Farmhouses at the Hida Minzoku-Mura Folk Museum

OLD WORLD—NEW WORLD

2 The heart of Tokyo at the central Ginza crossing

3 The Japan Alps at Kamikochi

MOUNTAINS AND SEA

4 A fishing village on the Okutango Peninsula

gentler with clothes than any western machine. Since nobody wears their clothes two days running, it does a good job. The electric ovens look efficient but the interior is tiny. Ovens are not used in Japanese cooking, but Japanese women have become keen bread- and cake-makers in recent years. The carpet shop holds a tremendous stock of western-style carpets but they are all cut into four standard sizes. How can one get a fitted carpet? Simple, as even the most modern apartment rooms are built to the traditional sizes of the old tatami reed mats, the basic unit of architectural floor measurement for centuries, and now applied to Wilton carpet. One complication is that there is one size of mat for Tokyo, another for the Kansai region, a special traditional size for Kyoto, and a new and smaller size for cheap modern apartments. Nothing is simple in Japan.

All I wish to do now is to sow seeds of doubt about the belief that Japan is wholly or largely westernised. The subject will come up again in different forms. At this stage it is enough to suggest the possibility that things are not as obvious as they may seem and one must not be deceived by appearances. In their way of using western objects, and in their attitudes to them, I think it will become clear that still, even among the young, these things exercise little real influence on the Japanese character and their deeper outlook on life.

Tokyo, as the former Edo, for 280 years the seat of the Tokugawa government, prompts another fundamental question about Japan. Again, it is an area where the apparent is misleading to the casual visitor. People travelling around Japan are struck by the large number of Shinto shrines and Buddhist temples everywhere, with many small shrines along the streets. If they enter a Japanese home, they will probably see a small Buddhist altar with an offering of rice for the ancestors, and a domestic Shinto shrine. If they are in Japan for one of the great festivals such as New Year, they will see Japanese flocking to their neighbourhood shrine, and on any day they may see the funeral rites elaborately observed outside the house where death has occurred. They may be confused to note that many Buddhist temples contain a Shinto shrine, and some shrines contain Buddhist objects.

From these observations people make two reasonable assumptions. First, they conclude that the Japanese are a religious people, even if following two obviously separate religions is perplexing. Secondly, they deduce that these two religions must still exercise a deep influence on Japanese society, ethically if no longer religiously. So the question is posed, 'Does Shinto or Buddhism have the greater influence on Japanese life?'

I think that neither Shintoism nor Buddhism exercise a deep influence on Japanese society. The dominant ethical influence remains the Confucianism that the Tokugawa government adopted and developed in the seventeenth century to underpin their political policy, now called neo-Confucianism. Although many Japanese seem largely unaware of the fact, they live in a basically Confucian society, based on neo-Confucian ethics and social principles. I will come back to Japanese religions and their significance. Here I want to concentrate on the continuing influence of Tokugawa Confucianism.

The subject must first be put into its historical context. Up to the late sixteenth century, no ruler had succeeded in subduing all the powerful provincial lords of Japan. For centuries the country had been torn apart by civil war. The ultimate desolation caused by these wars is epitomised in a letter that St Francis Xavier wrote in 1549 from Kyoto, where he described a flattened city of smoking ruins. But by the end of the century two exceptional generals had subdued the rebel lords, and in 1603 Ieyasu Tokugawa took control of an almost unified Japan. By 1615, after two more battles, Japan was united. From their new headquarters in Edo the Tokugawas now effectively controlled all of Japan, except for the north in which they had little interest.

The Tokugawas remained haunted by the fear of insurrection. They established a system of government which would minimise the chances of any local lord plotting against them. Each daimyo had to keep an establishment in Edo and live there for a statutory period each year. When he returned home, his wife and children remained in Edo as a guarantee for his good behaviour.

Slowly the Tokugawas created an intricate bureaucracy which attempted to regulate the lives of every citizen down to the colour of their clothes and the size of their umbrellas. The system was enforced with a network of government spies and frequent executions. As with all such bureaucracies, much of the regulation proved impossible to enforce. Their attempt to regulate social status, with samurai at the top and merchants at the bottom, was ignored as the merchants got richer, the samurai poorer, and the samurai were first forced to borrow money from the merchants and then to marry their children into the merchant families.

To support this new order, and to give it ethical credence, the government turned to the social teachings of Confucius, as reinterpreted by contemporary Japanese scholars, notably Ogyu Sorai (1666–1728), who extracted a social structure from Confucian ethics. Confucianism was long established in Japan. Prince Shotoku, drafting Japan's first constitution in the seventh century, had been inspired partly by Confucian models. Throughout the Middle Ages Japanese rulers took up and dropped both Confucianism and Shintoism in forming their policy. Thus Confucianism had a long and respected tradition in Japanese ethics and it gave respectability to the form of society the Tokugawas were trying to establish. This promoted the idea that the natural evil in man can be overcome only by good government and strong social institutions. Neo-Confucianism moved away from its earlier recognition of individualism to the idea that a man's prime identity sprung from his role in society. The group-oriented society was established in Japan.

In Edo times the dominant influence of Confucianism over Shinto and Buddhism was more obvious. Confucian scholars abounded, distinct in their regulated dress. There must have been a number of Confucian temples in Japan at that time. Today I know of only three, one in Tokyo, one in Nagasaki and a particularly fine one in Shizutani. The temple in Tokyo originally had a school for Confucian studies which became one of the forerunners of Tokyo University. Contemporary Japanese society is still heavily influenced by the neo-Confucianism of the Tokugawas and the society shaped by that political and ethical system, despite all the changes of the Meiji period, still underlies the whole social structure of modern Japan.

In Britain the Industrial Revolution brought about a complete break with the past early in the nineteenth century. So in Japan, the Edo period brought a new age and new attitudes to everything. Japan in the eighteenth century was as far removed from the world of Genji and Heian ideals as Victorian Britain was from Chaucer and medieval chivalry. Modern Japan must be interpreted mainly through the history of the last 350 years. In most respects it is the Edo period that still exercises the most fundamental influence. Japan remains primarily a Confucian society with a bureaucratic type of government directly inherited from Tokugawa tradition.

Today, when a 'company man' answers his office telephone usually he gives the name of his company before his own. In Japan his company is his prime identity. In neo-Confucian terms, his place in an ethical society is as a member of one of the recognised institutions which are the true components of a well-ordered society. The hierarchical structure of all Japanese society is based on Confucian teaching, with particular emphasis on the family as the basic unit of society. This is protected and regulated by a variety of ethical disciplines such as respect for seniority and old age, the dominant role of the male, and all the concepts and duties springing from filial piety and duty. Perhaps even Japan's recent 'examination hell' may be blamed partly on this borrowed Chinese philosophy.

It is typical of the difficulty of making judgements about Japan from appearances. Neo-Confucianism has no monuments to remind the observer of its importance. It lives on invisible, seldom mentioned, but woven into the fabric of Japanese society, while the casual observer sees only Buddhist temples and Shinto shrines.

Whether you are trying to estimate the degree of westernisation in Japan, or trying to analyse the influences that shape contemporary Japanese thinking, it is safer to presume that first impressions and external appearances are misleading. Never judge a restaurant by its exterior. Wait until you have eaten the food, and paid the bill.

The New Frontier

HOKKAIDO ISLAND

I have been to Hokkaido only once and I must admit that I was slightly disappointed. This was my own fault. I did not give myself enough time, only one week, and I did not plan my journey with sufficient care. It is a large and beautiful island, full of magnificent mountain scenery and unusual fauna and flora, but its size and general inaccessibility demand time. I would recommend anyone who likes nature to visit Hokkaido, provided they have time to do it justice, at least one to two weeks. I did enjoy the full glory of the Hokkaido autumn but if I returned, I would go in the winter. Hokkaido is a land for snow, from the beauty of the mountains to the fine ski-slopes, and the festival of snow-sculpture mounted each winter in the centre of its main city, Sapporo. After its wintry delights, the fresh Hokkaido summer also offers an escape from the oppressive heat and humidity further south.

Hokkaido's remoteness from the rest of Japan is reflected in the fact that it was established as an administrative area by the central government only in 1886. Today links grow closer as the island's prosperity increases, boosted by a large and all-year-round tourist industry and by a train tunnel, half completed, which will link it to Honshu. The most northerly of Japan's four main islands and uncomfortably close to the Soviet-occupied Sakhalin and Kurile islands, an endless cause of dispute between the two countries, Hokkaido is the second-largest island in the archipelago, having 22 per cent of Japan's land area, but only 5 per cent of Japan's population. In Hokkaido there is a distribution of 67 people per sq km in comparison with 5268 in Tokyo. By Japanese standards it is an empty place, a spacious new frontier.

Many Japanese like to dream of those wide open spaces but few move there.

Hokkaido keeps the last traces of Japan's earliest history, the people called the Ainu. The origins of the Japanese and their language are now becoming clearer. They seem to be a people who immigrated mainly from northern Asia, though there were probably also smaller migrations from other directions. The earliest Japanese records mention various groups of indigenous people, some of whom were probably the ancestors of the Ainu, driven north and by the nineteenth century mainly settled in Hokkaido and neighbouring islands. They, in their turn, must at some early period have come from the Asian mainland, though they are of a different racial type to the Japanese. They are characterised by the men's luxuriant head and facial hair which led them to be called 'the hairy people'. In 1878 the Ainu, in their language a human or man, were officially categorised by the government as *kyudojin*, somewhat contradictorily translated by my Japanese encyclopedia as 'former indigenous people'.

The Ainu are an interesting people with their own language, religion, culture and art, their artefacts and clothes decorated with distinctive patterns. They have no written language, but a strong oral tradition has preserved an enormous body of epic legends. From the late nineteenth century, when various Europeans stimulated interest in them, their culture and language have been carefully researched and recorded by Japanese scholars. It seems inevitable that the Ainu will vanish before long. Several thousand Ainu are still officially registered in Hokkaido – 24,000 in 1979 – but possibly as few as 10 per cent are pure blooded. Since the opening up of Hokkaido, disease and low birth-rate have continuously reduced the number of Ainu; and what hopes the remainder had of living a normal life has been jeopardised by their becoming a tourist attraction.

I visited one Ainu village museum in the south of Hokkaido and a forlorn place it was. The exhibits were interesting but the place had a predominantly commercial air. There were two Ainu houses, a small display of Ainu artefacts, and a large shop selling

Ainu souvenirs, roughly carved wooden mountain bears complete with salmon in their mouths and similar bric-à-brac. The saddest exhibits were an Ainu man and woman, the man with suitably flowing locks and a rather grubby but extensive beard, the woman all lacklustre and in ill-fitting Ainu robes. Their eyes had the apathy of all those preserved in 'reserves'. They were deprived of both their culture and their dignity. But nothing can be done to reverse the process. One feels in the presence of a terminal illness.

I liked everything about Sapporo, capital city of Hokkaido, an attractive, well-laid-out modern town, with a fresh, almost pioneering atmosphere and an exceptionally pleasant hotel. There are enough monuments to while away a day or two. There is the famous Clock Tower building, the only Russian-style building now left in the city, with a clock that has been ticking away since 1881. There is a good Ainu museum, botanical gardens and an interesting primeval forest covering Maruyama hill. I enjoyed wandering around the spacious streets and the uncrowded stores, looking at exhibitions of pottery and craftwork. One day I hope to see the February Snow Festival and the fantastic sculptures that are carved out of packed snow by the competitors. Apart from the fascination of seeing the Taj Mahal or Notre-Dame white and pristine in O-dori Park, I have a feeling that Sapporo would be at its best in mid-winter.

I managed to visit only two of Hokkaido's five national parks. I regret that I did not get up to the bleak northern coast where the Rishiri-Rebun-Sarobetsu Park takes in a stretch of the coast and two islands. A number of Japanese friends have praised the wild scenery there but have been less enthusiastic about the rough local boat journeys. I went first to Shikotsu-Toya, the national park just south of Sapporo. It is a beautiful area of lakes, mountains and volcanoes. Soft hills surround Lake Toya, small wooded islands floating on the clear waters, ruffled only by the busy little tourist-steamers. This is a volcanic area and the other major lake, Shikotsu, was formed by an eruption long remembered in Ainu legend. They deserted the area for fear of evil spirits.

More recently, and illustrating the resolve of Hokkaido people, was the eruption and rapid creation of the small mountain, Showa Shinzan, between 1943 and 1945. The stark contours of this mountain started in the winter of 1943 when an area of snow-covered land trembled and began to rise. The mound continued to grow until late in 1944. After several minor eruptions, the lava mound rose some 150 m until it finally stopped at 405 m. Many farmers abandoned the area early on, but the intrepid local postmaster stayed, photographing and studying every stage and eventually managing to buy the land occupied by the volcano. His studies were a unique contribution to volcanology, and in his will he left Showa Shinzan to the Japanese people. It remains a monument to Masao Mimatsu, and a reminder that everywhere in Japan people live daily with the threat of sudden natural disaster: typhoon, floods, volcanic eruptions and earthquakes.

Daisetsuzan National Park is the largest in Hokkaido and is in the centre of the island. I have special memories, particularly shame for my impatience with the not wholly exact map-reading of my companion on that occasion, Fumio. Fumio's sister is blessed with an unusually good sense of direction, which long ago got us around the narrow roads of Shikoku, but Fumio's sister was not with us on this occasion. Fumio suffered from the fault of many non-drivers. Peering earnestly at her map, she briskly snapped out orders like 'turn left' or 'turn right', unfailingly ten yards after we had passed the turning in question. It makes a driver testy but the fact is we always got there in the end.

It was late September, the height of autumn, which comes early in Hokkaido. We had golden days as we drove through the mountains burning with colour. Rushing streams glistened silver over the rock face which was framed in brilliant crimsons, golds, clear yellows and a patchwork of reddish-browns. Japan still waits for the painter with a genius to record its autumn. Colour photo-graphy lapses into the clichés of calendars and picture post cards. The Japanese autumn is my favourite season anywhere. It is little use talking to me about the fall in Massachusetts, or the autumn glories of the New Forest. I am openly prejudiced, convinced that those who have not enjoyed the autumn colours of Japan have missed one of the most ravishing sights in nature.

In the gorge of Sounkyo one is wrapped in autumn colouring as the wooded walls press tighter and tighter, the cliffs towering over the narrow road. In various places the formations of volcanic rock have led to names such as 'Big Box' and 'Little Box', while the waterfalls rejoice in such romantic names as 'Shooting Star' and 'Milky Way'. The Ainu believed in the magic of this enchanting place. They thought that the local fairies were skilled in weaving cloth of exquisite quality; perhaps spun from the magical colours of the autumn mountainsides.

I am no naturalist, and am always frustrated when I see obviously unusual or spectacular flowers and have no companion who can identify them for me. On the swaying seat of the ropeway that hauled us up the slope of Mt Asahi, below my dangling feet I saw not only a rich autumn carpet, but also a low undergrowth of dwarf bamboos and fascinating plants. Hokkaido is famous for its variety of alpine flowers and plants. They alone could be the purpose of a pilgrimage. I enjoyed the views from the mountain-top and came away with a sense of the richness of nature still unspoilt in Hokkaido, not least the home of the beautiful Japanese crane. Hokkaido certainly offers a place to get away from it all, and a glimpse of what so much of Japan must have looked like a century or even fifty years ago.

I call this chapter 'The New Frontier', for when the Japanese think of Hokkaido, it is a symbol of space, of an untamed land, of farms and ranches, a dream of nature unspoiled by industry or the speculator. To be truthful, most Japanese also think of the long, hard Hokkaido winter. But, despite that cold fact, Hokkaido offers spacious dreams. Most Japanese people, at every moment of their lives, suffer from lack of space which has become the most precious, and the most expensive, commodity in Japan. In many ways the Japanese have become inured to their severely crowded conditions; one could even say 'institutionalised', as now they seem to prefer to go with the crowd. Lack of space, and the lack of privacy that goes with it, has had a profound influence on Japanese life and social behaviour. The pressures have increased with the growth of urban life since the Meiji period, but traditional Japanese architecture suggests that part of the problem goes back to early times.

For those with no personal experience of Japan I will start with one example which not only emphasises the acute lack of space, but illustrates the way the Japanese learn to live with it. I was walking along Kyoto's main river. I crossed a bridge and there on the river bank, on a patch of sand roughly the size of a tennis court, nineteen Junior High School girls were playing tennis. There was no net, no lines and no surround. But the girls were all dressed in immaculate tennis dresses, had good rackets and were playing with total seriousness. One pair played from each corner, another pair from the centre. Three balls passed smartly between the six players on each base line, alternating their shots. It was tennis in several dimensions. Most surprising, the standard of play was high, with vigorous serves and strong forehand drives. The players seemed unworried by the lack of a net or line, and in the half-hour that I watched, not one ball went astray. For seventeen years I never missed a men's final at Wimbledon, but in a way that game on the banks of the Kamogawa river was the most memorable that I have ever seen.

Those river banks accommodate a bewildering variety of activities. I walked there every day and life by the river was an endless source of fascination. Mostly river banks are the preserve of young lovers. We had our share of those, extremely modest in their behaviour. I enjoyed the variety of sports and the winter kite-flying. More fascinating were the brass players, excluded from home, who gathered around one shrubbery while the woodwind were based on another. I have seen a complete set of drums set up in splendid isolation, the percussionist playing along with a vast tape-deck. There were Japanese Greek dancers and Japanese folk dancers, treading a measure amidst the fishing equipment scattered everywhere. Small boys paddled and pursued everything from tiddlers to crickets. There were trick-cyclists, dry-skiers, golfers, parties of elderly croquet fanatics, picnickers, firework parties and, strangest of all, usually around twilight, elderly men, poised at the water's edge, practising traditional forms of chanting. The wailing tones that echoed across the river on a quiet evening made it clear why there was no room at home for such activities.

The space we live in affects our daily lives both physically and psychologically. The physical size of a room controls our movements and the type of objects with which we surround ourselves. Also the room, and its relation to the other rooms in the house, control our privacy and influence our relations with others living with us. In the west we take our type of accommodation with corridors and individual rooms for granted. One can only understand the Japanese way of life if one realises that their most basic concepts about accommodation are different from ours.

I was travelling on a crowded bus one evening when three tired-looking schoolgirls got on, forced to stand with their heavy satchels. Their 'examination hell' was looming, they had not only put in a long day at school, but had put in another three hours at a cramming school. I felt sorry for them, but a Japanese friend pointed out that they had never known any other life. As they chattered amongst themselves, they seemed happy enough. Too often we judge others by our own needs.

Until fairly recently, the average household, whatever the size of the house, included two or three generations, increasing crowding and diminishing privacy. Up to the Second World War a great number of Japanese lived in reasonable-sized farmhouses and the individual could at least go out of doors to get away. The modern apartment, to which so many younger families are condemned, offers no easy escape. I lived for a number of years in a small apartment which would be described as: 6 + 4.5 + 8 DK. This equation equals one six-mat room (12 × 10 ft), one four-and-a-half-mat room (9 × 9 ft) and a dining/kitchen area of eight mats. It was very small and was designed for a newly married couple up to the time they were expecting a second baby. Then they would need to move. In an apartment of this kind one is seldom alone and in Japan children sleep with their parents. The 'love hotels' which have become an object of curiosity around the world are often used by married couples who have no privacy at home to make love.

Besides their apartments and small houses, the Japanese are crowded in the streets, on buses and trains, hemmed in at tightly packed, small tables of restaurants and coffee shops, and in compact rooms of hotels; and even at famous sightseeing places where the crowds flock to get away from it all. All this has a profound influence on Japanese behaviour. The Japanese may not require western-style privacy, but they do need and create a notional space around themselves into which they can withdraw and which in various ways is carefully respected by other people. The creation of this area and its protection help to explain a great deal about daily Japanese etiquette, general behaviour and deeper attitudes of mind. When faced with any problem about the Japanese, it is worthwhile to examine the enigma in terms of 'lack of space'. Often that will give at least part of the answer, even if several other factors are involved in the correct analysis of the complexities of social attitudes and behaviour.

Such a densely crowded society faces two special problems. There is the risk of various frictions destroying social harmony and even leading to violence. Also the individual's desirable personal development may be stifled. Much of the structuring of Japanese society is designed to overcome these problems. The individual is required to sacrifice much to sustain the general harmony. In return, society makes certain concessions to the individual. Society recognises that life is not easy for most individuals and is tolerant in providing small safety-valves, small indulgences, and defined areas of special freedoms. The permissive attitudes to smoking and mild drunkenness are typical.

The Japanese do not shake hands, and indeed avoid touching each other whenever possible. Even in a crowded street it is surprising how seldom people brush against each other, though some of the youngest generation are becoming less considerate. Mothers hug their children but seldom kiss them, and older children are hardly touched at all. When I first came to Japan I seldom saw anyone holding hands. It is now commonplace, but few Japanese have learned how to communicate through hand holding. It is mostly a western fad in which hands are limply linked. Couples seldom kiss in public. Kissing and love play are alien to the tradition of love-making but there are a growing number of exceptions. It is all neatly summed up in the Japanese saying that 'foreigners make love from the waist upwards'. The beautiful erotic prints of the eighteenth and nineteenth centuries confirm this attitude. Japanese ladies and gentlemen seldom bothered to undress before getting to it. Part of the explanation could lie in the difficulty of retying the elaborate sash of a woman's kimono.

The Japanese have developed special gifts of self-protection. Under the most distracting conditions they can sustain their powers of concentration. Offices are crowded. The average urban neighbourhood is noisy. But when one comments on such things, Japanese friends hardly notice them, and certainly waste little nervous energy fighting against them. They are masters at shutting things out, ignoring them, or simply dropping off to sleep under any conditions, including standing up in a packed commuter train. In these ways the Japanese preserve their identity, and maybe their sanity, in the frenzy of contemporary city life. All of this tends to drive the Japanese in on themselves and makes them a markedly introverted people.

The hierarchical structure of Japanese society, the emphasis on a person's group identity and status, the highly formal systems of behaviour and the intricacies of Japanese respect language can all be interpreted as measures to maintain harmony in an over-crowded society. The training for this disciplined way of life goes deep, so deep that at times it seems to override the basic needs and aggressions which control other human beings. A Swedish doctor I know worked for a time in a Japanese mental hospital. I asked him if he noticed any significant differences between Japanese and western mental patients. He thought that the strong discipline all Japanese receive remained effective even under considerable psychiatric stress. Patients remained calmer and, indeed, were expected to do so. Once, while his Japanese colleague was interviewing a girl patient, he asked her to look at some papers. The girl took the papers, read them and quietly tore them up. She was immediately removed to a hospital better able to cope with violent cases.

He also told me that there are two 'phobias' unique to the Japanese: some become obsessed that others are staring at them and become terrified of any eye-to-eye confrontation. In a crowded society it is an important obligation to be clean. Most Japanese do not sweat much, but a few do and can develop an imaginary obsession that they smell which can become traumatic for them. So, in a strange way, even mental health becomes part of the overall pattern and restraints of society.

The Japanese language, and the way it is used, helps to reduce possible frictions and provides further protection for personal privacy. In ordinary conversation charity towards others is a reflex action. One either says something kind or one says nothing. It is also impolite to express emphatic personal views or to push oneself forward in any way. While all this makes for harmony, it must be admitted that it can also make for boredom. But to the Japanese everything must be sacrificed for the sake of harmony, even the truth. In most ways the majority of Japanese are honest, but truth is more a convenience than an absolute and various forms of white lie are an essential part of Japanese life, particularly when they preserve the harmony and promote the welfare of the group.

3

Beyond the Barrier

NORTHERN HONSHU: TOHOKU

Even today some Japanese regard northern Honshu as remote and somewhat uncivilised, a hangover from earlier times when it was impossible to govern this area, and to maintain the barriers on the roads which strictly controlled all traffic in central Japan. There were moments while I was travelling in Tohoku when I began to share those feelings.

The railway official in the information office at Oguni station was all smiles. Our request seemed simple. We wished to know the time of the next train for Yamagata by the easterly line, which was clearly marked on my Japanese map.

The smiles faded into a kindly but distinctly professorial look. 'You cannot go that way. You must take the train up the coast via Sakata.'

That was exactly what I was trying to avoid. 'But I want to go east via Yonezawa.'

'I am afraid that is impossible. You must go via Sakata.'

'Impossible?'

'Yes, impossible, I am afraid. There is no railway line going east. You must go via Sakata.'

'But look, this Japanese map shows the eastern line.'

'I am sorry. I am afraid you have a very old map. It is much better for you to go by Sakata.'

'Excuse me, but it says this map was printed this year.'

'Ah so. Well, that railway line would not be suitable for you. You will find it more convenient to go via Sakata.'

'Forgive me, but how do you mean it would not be suitable? It's the way I want to go. Going by Sakata would be far more inconvenient.'

5 *Torii* of Itsukushima shrine on the shore of Miyajima at low tide

TRADITION—OLD AND NEW

6 The prefectural gymnasium at Takamatsu designed in 1964 by Kenzo Tange in the shape of a traditional fishing boat

7 Patterns of sand in Shokokuji Temple, Kyoto

NATURE WITHIN THE GARDEN

8 Reflections in water, a stone lantern to the right, in a private garden
in Kyoto

'The eastern line is too difficult for you. Please go by Sakata.'

'But I have this Japanese lady with me.'

'It would be too difficult for her. She is not familiar with this part of Japan. There is a train leaving for Yamagata via Sakata very shortly. You will find it most convenient. It will be very comfortable for you. It is an express train.'

'I know it's an express, but the journey by Yonezawa is much shorter.'

'That is quite true, but the Yonezawa train stops at many places. That will not be convenient for you. You will enjoy the express train. It will be more suitable.'

A street fortune-teller in Kyoto once told me, with considerable percipience, that stubbornness is the main feature of my character. We caught the train to Yamagata via Yonezawa, and it seemed to me comfortable, convenient and utterly suitable. The first twenty minutes of the journey, through the valley along the Mogami river, was magically afire with the colours of late autumn, as I had hoped. Unfortunately, our prolonged debate at the information office had so delayed our departure that tantalising darkness soon shrouded the view, leaving only the battlements of the surrounding mountains silhouetted against the night sky. We were chagrined that not only was this train comfortable, convenient and suitable, but also that the route was more beautiful.

In fairness I must add that this benign railway official was motivated only by a fatherly concern. The Japanese have rigid ideas about what is 'suitable', in this case the route favoured by the majority. The idea of a foreigner, even accompanied by a Japanese, risking life and limb on a branch line was not to be recommended. Indeed, it was to be resisted with every argument, sensible and senseless. I shall never know the potential discomforts, inconveniences and unsuitabilities of the Yonezawa route since miraculously we escaped them all. However, I know that to our would-be guardian angel they were utterly real. I am always charmed at how elderly Japanese officials tend to regard all foreign travellers, even those of some maturity, as nice but potentially mischievous schoolboys, requiring a certain avuncular discipline to protect them from their own capacity for folly.

Few foreigners visit Tohoku, particularly the most northerly part. That is a pity and I recommend this area where there are several interesting places and three magnificent national parks. Tohoku is less developed than much of Japan, but beware of guide-books that invite you into an older world. Tohoku has differences but they should not be exaggerated. Japan's general prosperity and modern development is now coming to Tohoku, helped by the opening of the new express Shinkansen railway from Tokyo. This is already ironing out regional differences. For the tourist, exploring Tohoku has been made much easier by the publication of an excellent and practical English-language guide (see Select Bibliography).

Tohoku, meaning 'north east', consists of the six northern prefectures of Honshu. The old name was Michinoku, 'back roads', and still today it is not difficult to get off the beaten track. In medieval times it was a feared place of exile, particularly for dissident noblemen and priests. It is said that these aristocratic exiles, banished from the refined court of Kyoto, wandered around this alien land bemoaning their fate in nostalgic courtly songs which are supposed to have left their influence on Tohoku folk music. There is a rich tradition of local songs, and the northern folk singers are considered among the best in Japan.

This is a rural area. Most of the towns are still small. The only large town is Sendai, administrative centre of the region and a busy, thriving city. Tohoku is characterised by natural beauty, and long, hard, snowbound winters. It is mountainous and these run from north to south dividing the colder Japan Sea coast from the rocky and spectacular Pacific seaboard. In three national parks sacred places lie hidden among volcanic mountains, lakes and tall forests. Basically the land is poor, but it has long been a granary for Japan and is now developing dairy farming.

Everywhere rural people tend to be the butt of national humour. Tohoku is no exception, and the 'Tohoku yokel' is a favourite figure of fun in television comedy. The people speak with a thick accent known as *zu-zu ben*. This is the subject of many jokes, all in line with Dorset yokels or Georgia crackers. They say the thickened speech is caused by the winter cold which forces the locals to speak with compressed lips. But behind the jokes, there is affection and admiration for these northern people. Their rugged way of life has given them determination and independence. To the foreign traveller they are kind and helpful, if initially surprised to find you in their part of Japan.

To suggest the character of Tohoku I have chosen five places I particularly enjoyed. Others might have made different choices. This is a large area with several interesting towns, a wealth of natural beauty, with a variety of folk crafts, traditions and some famous festivals. I can give only a flavour of the region in the hope that this may encourage others to explore for themselves.

My gateway to Tohoku was up the west coast into Yamagata prefecture. Immediately I began to look about trying to observe the differences I had been conditioned to expect as we entered the 'back country'. Was the landscape changing? Did the farms look poorer? Did people stare more? Was the standard of living lower, and was there a look of austerity in the people's faces? Nowhere in Tohoku were the differences as great as I had expected, though in the smaller towns and the countryside I did feel a general air of austerity compared to much of the rest of Japan.

From time to time I heard the thick *zu-zu ben*, from the station announcer, from two old men chatting in the bus. In the same bus, and elsewhere, the young girls and women seemed more plainly dressed than their fashion-conscious sisters further south, and on the whole the cars seemed older. Everywhere many faces had a rural look, a sturdy, farming people. As the local trains chugged through the narrow valleys, the small farmhouses were roughly constructed and one could see that these people lived a spartan life farming on that notoriously poor soil. As I passed by, life was warmed and brightened by the autumn sun. I thought of those valleys during the long, bitterly cold winters. A new prosperity is on its way to Tohoku but at present many people still lead a hard life.

Yamagata, prefectural capital, with a population of 209,000, is a small town by Japanese standards, but typical of the larger towns of Tohoku. The area in front of the railway station was characterless, concrete office blocks interspersed with a few coffee shops and business hotels. The city sprawls away into modern suburbs and the view to the north is enlivened by a line of mountains. There is no great air of prosperity and, compared to more sophisticated towns, the standard of dress is dull to dowdy. But like so many Japanese towns, in Tohoku and elsewhere, interesting places are hidden away which make a short stay well worthwhile.

Not far from the station, in the Kasumigajo Koen Park, site of the Mogami clan's now vanished castle, stands an unusual and charming relic of the early Meiji period. The Saiseikan Hospital and Medical School was built in 1878, presumably by a local carpenter (Plate 21). It is a reminder of Japan's new-found enthusiasm for both western things and western ideas, in this case architecture and modern medicine. It is a large, circular building fronted by an elaborate tower. The tiled roofs and oriental-latticed balconies are stylishly at odds with the western columns, the louvered shutters and the pink clapboard walls, and a touch of gothic in the fenestration. It rose up like some towering Regency folly, but even more reminded me of the architectural extravagances which resulted from the cotton boom in Natchez, Mississippi. Two years after the hospital was built, its westernisation was completed by the arrival of an Austrian doctor who came to teach western medicine. The building now houses a museum which tells its story. Originally the hospital was in a more central position, but to ensure its preservation it was moved to the park in 1965. There are a number of such hybrid pieces of architecture in the towns of Tohoku, all as charming as they are unusual.

Yamagata spread in recent years and its suburbs engulfed the pottery village of Hirashimizu. It would have been easier to find it by taxi but foolishly we went by bus. We got thoroughly lost, ending up on a mountainside by some huge, modern recreation centre with the compensation of a splendid view of the city.

Another bus and a short walk brought us to Hirashimizu, named after an old samurai family. It still retains a rural charm. The lanes wind between farmhouses and several potteries, though most of the buildings are not as old as they appear. A few of the potteries are famous, with prices to match. One or two specialise in simple, useful wares, which are attractive and cheaper. In many of these Japanese country potteries, always worth visiting, the tunnel kilns run up the steep hill behind, while in front a large building doubles as showroom and warehouse, for most of the pottery is sold elsewhere. We visited a pottery making a wide variety of table wares, some in a creamy-brown glaze, others like a delicate eggshell, a soft white speckled with flecks of green. I bought a set of tea bowls and the woman offered to pack and post them to Kyoto for an absurdly low price. The Japanese are not only master packers but have a magnificent system for dispatching parcels around Japan, much of it done by private companies. I have one other memory of that pottery. It was the only place in Tohoku where we met with rudeness. On the steps outside the showroom a group of men were sitting in the sun, gossiping. They barely moved as we tried to squeeze our way up the steps. Once it was obvious that we intended to buy something, we did receive more attention.

It is, however, a charming village. It is only a small area and at the end of the lanes one is suddenly in the country. But the pottery buildings, the rambling gardens around them, the old trees hanging over the walls and the general rural air are a delightful surprise after a long bus ride through the urban and suburban uniformity of Yamagata. All the potteries, more or less, welcome visitors. One pottery has exhibited all over the world and won prizes in Europe, but I preferred the simpler wares of Hirashimizu. I saw a number of potteries in Tohoku but this was the most interesting and by far the most attractive.

Yamadera is 13 km by train from Yamagata, a beautiful place of pilgrimage, where a temple was founded in 860 on the wooded slopes of Mt Hoju. It is a sharp but worthwhile climb to the top, and on a platform above the temple buildings is a splendid view across the neighbouring countryside. The path winds up among the trees and huge tumbled rocks. On the way one passes a statue commemorating the visit of the great Japanese poet, Basho (1644–94), by his wanderings patron of all travellers in Japan. He celebrated his journeys in seventeen-syllable poems called haiku, of which he was the great master. At Yamadera he wrote one of his most famous poems, contrasting the deep silence of the forest with the penetrating sound of the summer cicada. A book of Basho's poems makes an excellent travelling companion in Japan.

Some 60 km north-west of Yamagata is a magic place, perhaps among the five most beautiful and impressive places in Japan. Buddhism has produced strange sects, fierce asceticisms and esoteric practices. Dewa Sanzan is the sacred centre of the followers of the Shugendo esoteric sect, which combines elements of Shinto with Buddhism. The ancient province of Dewa contains three mountains sacred to this sect, Mt Gassan, Mt Yudono and Mt Haguro. Although Mt Haguro is the lowest at 419 m, it has most of the *yamabushi* buildings, as the members of this strange sect are popularly called. A road has now been built up Mt Haguro and most pilgrims glide to the top in limousine buses. But there is another, older way. I urge you to take it. The true pilgrims' ascent is by 2446 stone steps crawling in endless flights up the mountainside (Plate 18). I cannot claim to have counted them as all my breath was otherwise engaged.

Ikuyo was my guide and companion. She is reasonably energetic and always good-humoured. She had not been here before. Had she been, I suspect we would have taken the limousine bus. Fortunately, we were both facing the unknown. That day, although it was sunny, one could feel the first pinch of winter. We knew we had a considerable climb ahead of us. Ikuyo likes beer almost as much as I do, so we sat in a decrepit old village shop fortifying ourselves with beer and a snack of *konnyaku*, 'devil's tongue paste', made from a starchy root and eaten smeared liberally with hot mustard; delicious and warming.

The path to Mt Haguro led out of the village under the purifying gateway of a tall wooden Shinto *torii*. Down a steep flight of steps to the rushing river and we were at the edge of the forest. Across a rustic bridge and from then on it was up all the way, often the vista ahead 200 steps in a continuous flight. The forest was awesome as a gothic cathedral, its columns the ancient cryptomeria trees, its stained glass the glowing autumn colours caught here and there in shafts of sunlight, its music cascades and streams, its sacred atmosphere the deep shade and the silence.

It was a long and tiring climb. To the left, with dramatic suddenness, a deep vista opened up and at the end stood an old, many-storeyed wooden pagoda circled by the huge cedars, many over 300 years old. I was leading and without looking back I could sense that the distance between Ikuyo and myself was increasing. I took to pausing and the pauses grew longer as I waited for Ikuyo to climb another twenty steps. Just as I thought she was about to give up we came upon a small teahouse. We rested, drinking green tea and nibbling at more *konnyaku*, watched by a Japanese family fascinated to see a *konnyaku*-eating foreigner in this remote place. Looking out over the tops of the trees, in the distance, spread out in the sun, was the wide Shonai plain, one of the great rice-growing areas of Japan. Ikuyo, refreshed, determined to reach the top and we returned to the steps and the second half of the climb, eventually reaching the mountain top and the complex of temple buildings. It was one of those occasions when it was definitely better to travel than to arrive. After the magnificence of the forest, the temple was unimpressive and the precincts unpleasantly commercialised with the inevitable souvenir shops and ugly café. We waited for the bus, exhausted into silence but totally rewarded by the effort. I think Ikuyo had forgiven me.

Making this journey in the late autumn had the advantage that everywhere was uncrowded and it was easy to find accommodation without booking. On the other hand the official tourist season was over and everyone tended to tell us that we should find places closed for the winter. This rigid seasonal attitude to travel meant frequent struggles for Ikuyo and in Morioka, in Iwate prefecture, we received little encouragement to visit the Rikuchu-kaigan National Park on the Pacific coast. There were plenty of trains to

Miyako, the sightseeing centre, but we were warned that all tourist facilities were now closed.

Since my main ambition in coming to Tohoku had been to see this famous piece of coastline, I ignored these warnings. Thanks to Ikuyo's efforts we had little difficulty. In Miyako we found most things working and even a few Japanese tourists still enjoying the beautiful late autumn weather. Breakfast at our inn was enlivened by a group of Japanese men either celebrating their holiday, or applying the hair of the dog. They washed down their morning rice and pickles with enormous quantities of beer. They may have thought the season was over in Morioka, but we knew differently in Miyako.

The coast is of great beauty and my only regret is that we did not have time to see more, though the stretch around Miyako is a superb introduction. We took a bus a few kilometres north where we walked through a busy fishing port and out along the cliffs. Here we had our first view of the fascinating rock-sculptures, carved by wind and sea. The cliffs running north up the coast are sheer and impressive. The sea is scattered with small islands and gnarled rocks, in beautiful or fantastic shapes. From our viewing point we looked down on a curved and massive pillar of rock that thrust up out of the foaming spray, its rugged outline softened on the top by a few pines twisted by the wind. Water, rock and trees are the essential elements of nature in Japan. Yet in thousands of landscapes it is the spreading pine that makes the view unmistakably Japanese.

There was no bus back into town for over an hour and it was growing cold. In a corner of the harbour we found a tiny general store, owned by a very old lady. Her husband had deserted her many years before. Since then the shop had been her life. We sat drinking coffee and talking to her. She opened the shop seven days a week. As she greeted each fisherman who dropped in to buy cigarettes, or the children sent to purchase small items, it was obvious that she knew everyone. This small neighbourhood was her entire world. Her quiet acceptance of her circumscribed life was typical of her generation. She assured us a number of times that in her opinion the old ways were the best ways.

The next morning we took a boat excursion around the famous neighbouring Paradise Beach. We passed various attractive islands and grotesque rock formations washed by the boiling surf. A cloud of black gulls swept past the boat, screaming as they dived to snatch food from the fingers of the passengers. The rising cliffs, reaching 300 m in places, remind one of the great depth of the Pacific east of Japan, stretching away to the Mariana Trench, deepest place in the oceans of the world.

Going south, we came to Sendai, prefectural capital of Miyagi, and one place whose growth and prosperity is obvious. Everywhere shops were selling the famous traditional cast-iron kettles and cooking pots for which the area has long been famous. The old craft has been ingeniously extended. I found a charming small bird which at first I took for a piece of decorative sculpture. On closer examination I saw that its flared tail was in fact a bottle-opener.

Most delightful are the local painted wooden dolls, *kokeshi*, which are made in a limitless variety of sizes and designs, though always cylindrical in form. Said to have first been carved by poor workmen for their children, they caught the eye of the first tourists to the area and since have spread all over Japan, among the most pleasing of all Japanese folk objects.

Not far north of Sendai, just back into Iwate prefecture, is the small town of Hiraizumi. A short bus ride from the station is Chusonji temple, and one of the most fabulous art objects in Japan; in a way one of the most precious pieces of miniature architecture in the world. I dreamed of seeing it for fifteen years. It was quite different from what I had expected, but in no way disappointing, far excelling anything I had imagined. The Fujiwara family, who exercised great power in medieval Kyoto, had a large fortress at Hiraizumi from about 1090 to 1189. They ruled the area in great splendour, but the remains of the fortress are now of little more than archaeological interest. Scattered across a nearby mountainside are the many buildings of Chuson-ji temple, set prettily among the trees, more picturesque than important. The world comes to this place to see one thing, the *Konjiki-do*, the Golden or Glittering Hall, a translation that may suggest its magnificent decoration, but not the small scale of the structure which is only 5.5 m square. This miniature Buddha Hall was built between 1109 and 1124, and is a mausoleum for three Fujiwara lords. Paved and walled with gold, in the centre is a raised altar, enclosed by four circular pillars. On the altar are eleven serene Buddhist deities. Every surface is decorated and enriched with delicate patterns worked in ivory and mother-of-pearl. The quality is breathtaking, like some exquisite reliquary. In its golden magnificence, it represented to the followers of the Judo sect the 'Western Paradise'. There seems to be an influence of T'ang China, its precious and exotic materials and elements of the decorative designs brought along the Silk Road. It also reminds us that Tohoku was not wholly without civilisation in the medieval period. In the darkness of northern Japan Hiraizumi was an outpost of Heian culture, often called the 'Mirror of Kyoto'.

In the remoter parts of Tohoku to a slight extent life still recalls an older Japan where an underlying poverty ingrained thrift into the Japanese character, together with frugality. These characteristics are rapidly vanishing as increasing materialism transforms Japanese life. Recently I was talking to a well-known Japanese mountaineer, in his late thirties and from Tohoku. It was obvious that he thought the younger generation were pampered and spoilt. Certainly their public behaviour, and their unhealthy complexions do not contradict him. But he is a typical Tohoku man, and while the Japanese may ridicule these northerners on television, the people of the 'back country' in turn look down on their southern compatriots. As everywhere, the poor have their own pride.

Until after the Second World War and the 'economic miracle', Japan had been a poor country. With few natural resources, at every level austerity was the mother of invention. In the most northern prefecture of Aomori, in earlier times, cotton was so scarce that the farmers were forbidden to wear cotton cloth. They dressed in rough hempen garments, but since plain cotton thread was available, to make the hempen cloth stronger and a trifle warmer, the women stitched the hemp with cotton. Soon this stitching formed into intricate patterns and a new folk art was born, popular to this day.

Poverty and making do was for centuries the basic pattern of life for most Japanese. For hundreds of years rice was precious and was the currency in which the lords paid their samurai. The ordinary Japanese subsisted mainly on rougher grains such as barley. These centuries of deprivation left a mark on the Japanese character. People retain a special respect for rice and dislike throwing away any food. Look inside the refrigerator of any more traditionally minded Japanese and you will find it crammed with plastic bags holding remnants of food which will be used up in future meals. But as Japan moves forward into the age of 'instant noodles' and fast-food restaurants where even the traditional *o-sushi*, raw fish on rice balls, circulates on a conveyor belt, attitudes will change and the thrifty housewife will be an exception.

In Tohoku, and other parts of Japan, there are areas where the 'economic miracle' has not yet arrived to raise people from a subsistence level. Some Tohoku men are forced to come south to work as day-labourers on building sites. It's a hard and lonely life where the day ends in a cheap doss-house or the site's dormitory and cheap sake is the only escape from the hard realities of life. Many of these men are splendid characters, almost contemporary samurai. In flared 'jodhpurs' and brightly coloured belly-bands, they strut about the streets with great panache. Although many of them look brutally tough, the few times I have stopped one to ask the way, I have found them polite and full of humour.

The influence of scarcity and thrift has not only influenced the poor. Throughout earlier Japanese history even the nobility led a more spartan life than their western peers. A great fascination of Japanese art and architecture is its ability to make so much out of so little. A discipline, based on thrift, has maintained a wonderful respect for the raw materials. Craftsmanship, with incredible ingenuity, has created a highly sophisticated culture out of the simplest elements: clay, bamboo, lacquer, paper. This same ingenuity is now at work in the fields of electronics and the microchip. Devices and gadgets invented in the United States or Europe take on new dimensions when developed by this peculiarly Japanese form of creativity. The electric coffee-making machine was obvious, but it took the Japanese to build in a coffee-grinder. The electronic typewriter is already familiar, just as the portable typewriter has been around for years. But it took the Japanese to devise the portable world-processor with nearly every function of a full-sized machine, weighing in at little over 2 kg. I have just seen the latest model, no larger, but now capable of typing not only the Roman alphabet with variations and accents for every European language, but also the 100 characters of the two Japanese phonetic alphabets and the 2000-odd *kanji* Chinese characters, of which hundreds consist of over twenty strokes. Yet some still argue that the Japanese are not creative.

There is no doubt that a great wave of materialism is now destroying the qualities typified by the simpler life of Tohoku. It is, however, difficult to get Japan's economic miracle into perspective, particularly how it has affected the average individual. Whatever the international press may say, not every wallet in Japan is bulging. Without question, for the mass of people life is much better than it was before the Second World War. More Japanese travel abroad, more own cars, the department stores are cornucopias of foreign goods and the leading companies make handsome profits. To the outside world the cake looks big, but from inside it is by no means equally sliced. Without doubt the economic growth has slowly brought a higher standard of living to most people, and an enormous improvement to those who can remember pre-war conditions. Japan's national wealth has raised individual standards of living and provided excellent public services and facilities, whether it be trains or shopping. Japan's economic success has brought great wealth to a small number, though surprisingly the annual published list of top taxpayers always includes more land speculators, doctors and dentists than leaders of commerce and industry. Many company chairmen, even in the highest positions, receive salaries that are modest compared to their equals in the United States or Europe.

Looking around my own Japanese friends, typical of Japan's predominant middle class, middle managers, research workers, teachers, university professors, local government officers, I get the impression that all of them have to be careful to make ends meet. Recently I had a letter from the wife of a young doctor, worrying that the obligatory expenses caused by the marriages of two close relatives had seriously upset her quarterly housekeeping budget. Last week the wife of a young company man, both in their early thirties, was staying with me. In every way it was obvious that she had to count every yen to make her husband's meagre salary meet Tokyo's high cost of living. And when her first child arrives, the budget will get much tighter. The suicide rate in Japan is high, and it is significant that many suicides each year result from those caught in the terrible web of the loan-sharks. Some may have got into debt through heavy gambling, but there are plenty of sad cases where a father has gone under struggling to give his daughter a worthy wedding.

So who is spending all the money in these magnificent department stores? Who, in these Aladdin's caves of international fashion, can afford such luxury goods? The first answer is the young, particularly unmarried men and women earning reasonable salaries but still living at home. The Japanese call them the 'young aristocrats'. Like their kind the world over, they have money in their pockets and few responsibilities on their minds. Apart from them and the genuinely rich, Japan has a vast population. If each person treats themselves to one or two luxury items each year, that adds up to a lot of goods. Older women, once the family has left home, are slightly better off. Evidently, even in the more rural areas, such women are demanding such luxuries as foreign fashions and French perfume. For those who cannot afford the genuine article, there is a brisk trade in fake 'European' handbags and other accessories, manufactured in the backstreets of Osaka, or sneaked in from Hong Kong.

The old tradition of thrift is dying in Japan. The worst kinds of western materialism are developing, bringing with them the familiar symptoms of crime, corruption, debt, and a rash of juvenile delinquency. Long deprived of the riches of the world, the Japanese sometimes seem like children let loose in some fantastic, international toyshop. But I doubt if many Europeans would exchange their own way of life for this seeming prosperity. The gleaming Toyota must be squeezed into a minute parking space in front of a miserably small and poorly built house or apartment. For most people the 'economic miracle' is living with two small children in one cramped living room in which the metre-wide kitchen area is ill concealed by a lace curtain, and the preparation of each meal is a balancing act. Up a staircase as steep as a European loft-ladder are two tiny bedrooms.

Amongst the clutter of life and the children's toys, the Paris umbrella or the Italian handbag are the tiny treats that punctuate the long day, the endless patience and forbearance and, with months of pinching on the budget, a four-day summer holiday. They read daily, not without some bitterness, of the bribery and corruption commonplace among the rich and the politicians, and of the frequent vast tax evasions by doctors and dentists. For the huge new middle class of Japan things are better than they were, but for several that I know life is by no means easy. The 'economic miracle' does not always seem so immediately miraculous to the majority of Japanese.

4

From Factory to Fuji

EAST CENTRAL HONSHU: KANTO AND KOSHINETSU

This large area covers nine prefectures and includes Tokyo. The title of this chapter tries to suggest the variety and contrasts to be found here, from the vast industrial development around Tokyo to the magnificence of the Japanese Alps to the west, and the gentler beauty around Mt Fuji to the south. Each prefecture has some notable features, old or modern. There is the silk production of Gunma, the unique Shinto mausoleum of Tochigi, Japan's first atomic power plant in Ibaraki, the controversial Narita International Airport in Chiba, the ancient splendours of Kamakura in Kanagawa, and Japan's heaviest snowfalls in Niigata. Here I can do no more than describe a few favourite places. Each place has its own character, but I could not pretend that the selection is wholly representative of this multi-faceted area, as packed with natural beauty and historic monuments as it is with modern scientific and industrial marvels, such as the growing 'Science City' at Tsukuba.

The 'Romance Express' from Tokyo's Asakusa station in two hours hastens you 140 km due north to the mountainous countryside of Nikko. Here there is a choice between one of the most outstanding pieces of architecture in Japan and some exceptionally beautiful walks among the lakes and waterfalls of the mountains above Nikko. To do the area any justice you should stay two nights. This offers the opportunity of staying the first night at one of Japan's few old western-style hotels, near the great shrine. The Edwardian-style public rooms contrast nicely with the public baths, labelled 'Wistaria', 'Azalea' and other flora with romantic Japanese associations. The second night you can enjoy the comforts and French cooking of a modern, alpine-style hotel, hidden away at the far end of Lake Chuzenji. Amongst various facilities, they offered bikes for dwarfs at giant rental charges.

Not far from Nikko station is the great Shinto shrine and the mausoleum built for Ieyasu Tokugawa, first shogun, in 1634–6, following his own instructions. The shrine is set among a forest of cedars, and no expense was spared in its construction and extravagant decoration. The best craftsmen were brought from all over Japan, particularly from Kyoto and Nara. It was probably the influence of the latter which caused the design to be in the rich style of the Momoyama period. Tradition has it that 2,489,000 sheets of gold leaf, each 25 cm square, were used, while the lengths of timber would stretch 530 km. But such statistics do little to conjure up the sumptuousness of the shrine, its drum tower and belfry, the store houses and sacred stables, and two fairy-tale gateways encrusted with dragons and quaint figures. The name of the 'Twilight Gate' warns that once we look upon it, its beauty will hold us until darkness falls. The overwhelming richness of the shrine with the glitter of gold, the polychrome colours of the carved and pierced panels and the sweeping elegance of its great roofs is given a deeper beauty and a quieter harmony by the more sombre background of the surrounding dark cedar forest.

Twenty kilometres west, one climbs into the mountainous area by two unusual roads, one for the ascent, the other for the descent. One road has twenty-eight hairpin bends, the other twenty, the forty-eight equalling the Japanese classic alphabet from which the roads are named *Irohazaka*. At the top is a wide plateau filled largely by Lake Chuzenji, 21 km in circumference. There are several fine waterfalls around the lake, the most famous being the 100-m Kegon Falls. My favourite, at the far end of the lake, is the 'Dragon Head Falls'. A large rock divides the flow of water creating a double falls. I visited these falls five times on various tours. We gazed for five minutes from the viewing platform, took our photographs, snatched a cup of coffee and were hustled back onto the bus. We had 'done' the 'Dragon Head

Falls'. When my elder son, who is a keen mountaineer, first came to Japan, we visited Lake Chuzenji. We walked to the falls and looked at the sparkling 'façade' from the conventional viewing place. Any slope going upwards is irresistible to my son. Within seconds he had disappeared up the edge of the falls. There was no need for mountaineering feats since he discovered a path which wound up behind the falls and followed the stepped river full of huge rocks which ran down the mountainside in a series of sparkling falls.

Beyond the road at the top, the river shrank and meandered through wide marshes which spread out to the surrounding mountains. This marvellous vista tempted us to rent a car. The next day we followed the winding road rising beyond Chuzenji. After 15 km we stopped and looked back. It was a breathtaking and huge landscape. Between the mountains on either side, the land dropped down to Lake Chuzenji in a series of steps, and on each plateau was another lake making a chain of silver sheets of water, the sun sparkling each surface. The whole area is full of good walks, an abundance of wild flowers at certain seasons, and the pleasures of solitude once away from the tourist centre at the east end of Lake Chuzenji.

South of Nikko is the famous pottery centre of Mashiko. In recent years it was made more famous as the home of the great Japanese potter, Shoji Hamada, one of the founders of the '*Mingei* Movement' which did much to revitalise Japanese folk crafts. Since his death, Hamada's home has become a museum. There was a strange irony in Hamada's life. He preached the virtues of the humble, anonymous folk craftsman, and all his life refused to sign his work. Despite this, he became the richest potter in Japan and far from being anonymous, became one of the most famous potters in the world. I once spent a delightful autumn day with him at Mashiko. We sat in the sun talking while he decorated piles of plates with quick, and always original, strokes of his brush. Just before we left, he took myself and two companions into a small building lined with pieces of his work. He invited each of us to select one piece as a memento of our visit. However, when I suggested that he might scribble his signature on the base, he just gave me a wry smile.

Kanagawa Prefecture, immediately south of Tokyo, has two historic towns, although of very different periods. Kamakura, one hour from Tokyo, is the most interesting old city in Japan after Kyoto. In 1192, after centuries of strife in Kyoto, a military government was formed which established a second 'capital' at Kamakura, removed from the intrigues of the Imperial Household and the menace of the powerful Buddhist temples of Kyoto. The Kamakura period lasted until 1333, and the martial spirit of the times, together with the establishment of Zen Buddhism, exercised a great influence over the art and architecture of the period. Kamakura occupies a beautiful site by the sea, a bay surrounded by wooded hills. At first little more than a village, it grew to be a great city, full of large temples and other buildings. Later much of the town was destroyed, but enough remains to make it worth a visit. The 40-ft-high seated bronze Buddha, cast in 1252 for the Kotokuin Temple, would alone make a visit worthwhile. The temple was swept away by a tidal wave in 1495, but the 93-ton figure remained, more effective for its unusual open-air site. It is a miracle of early bronze casting, and a great work of art. It is amazing that such a huge figure can express such spiritual calm, both the pose and the gentle face suggesting an inner strength. Kamakura has a number of fine Zen temples, notably Engakuji and Kenchoji. Crowds also flock to the large Hachimangu Shrine, whose approaching avenue runs through the centre of the modern town. I first came here in the pouring rain and nearly had a bad fall trying to race over the wet slope of its steep and famous drum-bridge. Within the shrine there is an enormous ginko tree which may be the oldest and largest in the world. Beyond these well-known sights, Kamakura could offer days of sightseeing and is underrated by most visitors.

Little remains in the great modern port of Yokohama to recall the foreign settlement opened there in 1859, only five years after Commodore Perry and his small American fleet had 'persuaded' the Japanese government to start opening Japan to the rest of the world. Today an excellent museum and library, housed in the old British consulate, record those colourful days when Yokohama boasted its own *Punch*-style magazine and the crinolines of the western ladies were the wonder of the Japanese. Today, the bustle of early Yokohama lives on only in the delightful Japanese prints showing the strange life of the foreigner.

Diagonally opposite, in the north-west corner of this region, is the large town of Niigata, prefectural capital of Niigata, and the port for Sado Island. Although small, Sado is the fifth largest island in the Japanese archipelago. The crossing took three hours to the small port of Ryotsu. Sado Island has an interesting if gloomy history. For centuries it was Japan's island of exile. Political trouble-makers and turbulent priests, those too important to execute, were banished to this bleak place. The most famous exile was the great Buddhist reforming priest, Nichiren, who lived on Sado from 1271 to 1274. But while these men suffered loneliness, at least they enjoyed a limited freedom on the island. Later exiles were less fortunate. In 1601 gold was discovered in the mountains at Aikawa. Throughout the Edo period the mines were worked by prison labour, working under conditions of misery and hardship that frequently led to death. In recent times the mines have been largely exhausted, but an excellent museum has been created in a section of the original shafts and galleries which recaptures the dreadful life of the prisoners.

Maybe it was such historical memories, maybe the dying autumn, but there seemed a melancholy about Sado despite the beauty of its seascapes and the views across the central plain. The towns had a kind of austere dignity, all along the country roads were fine old farmhouses and everywhere the people were kind. On our first night, trying to find our lodging in the darkness and cutting wind, we got completely lost and went into a garage to ask directions. A man filling his car overheard our problem and immediately insisted on driving us to our pension. The owner was a sweet woman with a great toothy smile who cooked a variety of delicious fish for our supper. My other memory is more bizarre.

In a Ryotsu back street we passed a large hoarding mounted on the wall of a Buddhist cemetery (Plate 26). Lurid and nakedly suggestive posters advertised the week's offering at the cinema opposite. I never cease to marvel at Buddhist tolerance, but I doubt if Nichiren would have approved.

If the Japan Alps are not on your itinerary, then I urge you to amend it. Mountaineers will choose their own time, but for the ordinary sightseer I recommend the late autumn when the early snows crest the autumn colouring (Plate 3). There are three ranges of Japan Alps, first so named in 1881 by an English engineer called William Gowland. The term was popularised by the English missionary, Walter Weston, who introduced mountaineering to Japan. The best gateway to the Alps is through the charming town of Matsumoto, and on up to Kamikochi, an ideal centre for walking and climbing.

There is little that is alpine about Matsumoto though it does have the air of a busy tourist centre. Opposite the station is a fine new shopping centre, bulging with food, women's fashion and an enormous bookshop. Such complexes suggest that most Japanese spend their money on food, clothes and books and magazines, in that order. Apart from shopping, Matsumoto has two architectural attractions. In the centre of the town, in an attractive garden and surrounded by part of the old moat, is the early seventeenth-century castle. Like most Japanese castles, it has been restored since the Second World War, but its black wooden walls, the six-storeyed donjon and the elaborate tiled roof give it the romantic appearance of a fortified pagoda.

Nearby is a charming old school, recently moved to this quiet site. The Kaichi school was built in 1876 by an ingenious local carpenter in his personal Meiji 'baroque' style. The main block and the windows are of almost classical simplicity and excellent proportions. But this soberness is enlivened by a charming octagonal turret, complete with a railed balcony. The entrance portico is unashamedly Japanese in taste, boldly carved with cloud scrolls and a writhing dragon. However, two impudent and distinctly western putti crown the ensemble, stretched between their pudgy hands a scroll bearing the name of the school in Chinese characters. The interior is cool and elegant with a handsome central staircase and a large assembly room upstairs. Now a museum, the early days of the school are illustrated by notebooks, drawings and handiwork of the Meiji pupils. It seemed sad that the school was not still used.

We decided to break our journey to Kamikochi. I am glad that we did as otherwise we should never have experienced the Pension Shirufurei. Pension is now a Japanese word, and a uniquely Japanese institution; in no way related to those gloomy places that highbrow aunts used to recommend, all lace curtains and congealed pasta. The Japanese pension is a newish type of accommodation, designed mostly for swinging young girls, who in Japan tend to holiday with other swinging young girls and are found mostly in tourist resorts. They cultivate a homely atmosphere. While the owner plays a double role of host and entertainer, his wife cooks food that is usually exceptionally good and original in style. It is all deeply Japanese.

Pension Shirufurei was my introduction to these delights. If you are puzzled by the name, so was I. Even after I had had difficulty in getting through the front door through the barricades of rabbits, still the penny did not drop. A rabbit on the door mat, rabbit stickers all over the entrance hall walls, rabbit mugs on a table, and in the 'common room' there was a mountain of large stuffed rabbits. To fit a western word to Japanese phonetic spelling drastic changes must often be made. The vagaries of *katakana* English, the abundance of rabbits and a word from our host gave me the clue. I was in the Japanese land of *Watership Down*, in that place of repose, 'Silflay'. Our host and his wife had been told about the book, and though they had not read it, they had in their Japanese way made it the theme of their pension.

When I got to my comfortable bedroom, inevitably it was another rabbit warren. There were even rabbits on the slippers. None of this surprised me. It only recalled all my girl students, aged mostly twenty-two or twenty-three, who came to class each day draped with pink, quilted shoulder-bags, embroidered with such sentimental exhortations (always in English) as, 'Let Us Enter Fairyland', or 'Friends with Kitty', or 'Taste The Candy Life'. Grammar and syntax were no part of these messages, but the cult expanded into Snoopy pencil cases, Mickey Mouse badges, a variety of pretty tags and tinkling bells, often attached to a smart Paris handbag, and the ensemble completed by pink sneakers and white socks with frilly lace edges, suitable for toddlers anywhere else in the world.

Japanese society is largely successful in controlling its young unmarried girls by keeping them in an extraordinary nursery world, of which the Pension Shirufurei is part. I do not write this in a spirit of criticism. It has its own charm, and a serious social purpose. If you find it all absurd, remember that, in general, Japanese girls can walk anywhere without being molested, and that millions of girls enjoy this kind of game. It would not work anywhere else. But it works in Japan. In China they used to bind girls' feet. In Japan society attempts to bind girls' minds.

I enjoyed my stay at the Pension Shirufurei enormously. It was very comfortable and the food was original and delicious. Pension life centres on the 'common room', equipped with books, games and a stereo. After supper it is customary for the host to hold a get-together when the guests are introduced to each other, having up to that moment, in a very Japanese way, studiously ignored each other. Our energetic young host, Pinocchio with a blunted nose, set the two Japanese couples at ease with each other, and with the elderly foreigner who had intruded into their magic kingdom. We sat up late talking about life in Japan. Despite our lateness to bed, our host's breakfast was as excellent as his supper.

I have been to the Hakone area and Mt Fuji many times. I have seen Fujiyama from the train and from aircraft, and usually I have seen only cloud. I first saw Mt Fuji from the roof of a warehouse in Tokyo, but I have also seen it serenely reflected in the waters of the Five Lakes. I have seen it floating in a mantle of cloud, and I have seen its gentle cone pristine against a blue sky. Always I have felt the magic it has exercised for centuries over the Japanese imagination.

Hakone is an area of great beauty. On my first visit I stayed in a charming Japanese inn at a hot-spring resort called Miyanoshita. In those days the better inns still provided each guest with a maid. That poor girl, what a shock I gave her. She saw me to the bath, removed my western clothes and left me with a cotton kimono. After my bath, following western male practice, when I put on the kimono, I folded it right over left. My little maid took one look, screamed, and rushed at me tearing at the front of the kimono. In Japan, only the dead wear the kimono folded that way.

My most vivid memory of the Fuji-Hakone area is another of those uniquely Japanese occasions, an evening in a cheap *robata-yaki* restaurant, near Tokai University. Its main claim to fame is the production of many of Japan's judo champions. A Swedish doctor friend was studying psychiatry at the university hospital and was friendly with a Korean girl studying at Tokai. Although it was deep winter and there was a lot of snow, we decided to go by the mountain train from Odawara to the Hakone Open Air Sculpture Museum. More an old-fashioned tram than a train, the two cars struggled up the steep tracks, through long, black tunnels, past the small stations and through a white crystal landscape of snow-covered pines and undergrowth. In the distance the mountains of Hakone lay under the shadow of heavy clouds promising more snow. It was a landscape of winter silence. On arrival we discovered that icy conditions had closed the museum. By the time we got home, cold, wet feet and a rather inadequate lunch had given us all a splendid appetite, and thirst. The general vote was cast for the ample food of *robata-yaki*.

Japanese restaurants, cheap or expensive, tend to specialise in certain types of cooking, partly because the type of food may dictate the layout of the restaurant. Some Japanese foods are best eaten sitting at a counter because they must be eaten as soon after cooking as possible, and they are served almost mouthful by mouthful. They are my favourite type of Japanese restaurant, a *sushi* bar with iced beer for summer lunch, *robata-yaki* with warm sake for a winter evening. The food and drink have a special quality and one's pleasure is heightened by the relationship between the clients and the cooks.

That night was cold and slushy with a cruel wind cutting down from the mountains. The cheap restaurant welcomed us with warmth and a gentle murmur of conversation. A scrubbed, white wooden counter surrounded a large grill. On the slope behind leant flat baskets of meat, fish and a variety of vegetables. The atmosphere was compounded of heat, teasing smells, smoke from the grill and the subdued chatter of three waiters who served the customers, who preferred to sit at the tables around the walls. The food was excellent, the sake comforting. But the evening was made by the commanding presence of the head cook. He alone served those of us seated on stools at the counter. He stood behind the wide grill, tall and gaunt, sweat glistening on his bared chest. A tightly twisted green towel snaked around his shaven skull. His eyes stared ahead, empty yet angry, his face devoid of humour, his body balanced, each movement economical. His hands worked precisely, flicking slabs of meat or slices of squid onto the hot grill, each piece of fish or sliver of vegetable dabbed or smeared with the necessary oil, sauce or scattering of salt. Octopus, beef, whale, egg plant, potatoes, needle fish, mushrooms, peppers, sweetcorn, each were flipped and tossed with long steel chopsticks. When cooked, the pieces were deftly placed on a narrow wooden paddle and passed out to the customer. I enjoyed the evening for the good food and drink, but best for the memory of that strange, green-bandannad, Zen-style cook. Like a jigsaw, the Japanese character is made up of many strangely shaped pieces.

Even in this exceptionally homogeneous, close-knit and conventional society, there is no such person as the 'average Japanese'. In recent years, as young people have enjoyed more freedom and started to glimpse the outside world, one finds a greater variety of attitudes and life-styles in Japan. Almost weekly I am reminded of this as I meet new Japanese acquaintances and make new friends. Within a narrow range there is a growing variety. In the last three months a number of Japanese have stayed a night or two here, a middle manager, a girl teaching in a special school for the deaf and dumb, a young Tokyo housewife, a High School physics teacher and his family, a man who works in an electronics company but who in his spare time farms the family rice fields, and a young Japanese surgeon who had just returned from a year in an American hospital. All were under forty and all had much in common, more than they would probably realise. But one should not ignore their differences and in some of them a growing objectivity about Japan. In their differences and a budding individuality lie some clues to the future of Japan. Admittedly, they were all exceptional simply in the fact that they were staying with a foreigner. In a recent opinion poll some 70 per cent of Japanese stated that they had no wish to meet foreigners. There are times when I can hardly blame them.

However, I have invented an 'average' young married couple, Mr Haruo and Mrs Misako Sato, to enable me to give a general picture of Japanese daily life and some of the common attitudes that control it. Perhaps 'compiled' would be more accurate than 'invented', for the Satos' life is entirely drawn from real experiences and incidents that I have known, a creation of fact rather than fiction. It is a device, but I hope to avoid undue distortion.

Haruo and Misako were both born in a town on the Inland Sea near Okayama. Misako came from an exceptionally conservative family, but she was intelligent and independent. She did well studying English literature at university and, by doing part-time work in coffee shops, saved enough money to attend a three-month summer school overseas in Oxford. This experience increased her feeling of independence and, resisting her mother's wish for her to get married, she found a job in Tokyo where she lived for fifteen months. Returning home for the New Year holiday, as she was approaching her twenty-sixth birthday, she knew that her mother would increase the pressure for marriage. She was hardly through the door when her mother told her excitedly that a close friend, not a professional go-between, had recommended a charming and suitable young man and a marriage meeting had been arranged in three days' time.

Misako accepted the inevitable, particularly as the recommendation had come from a close friend, and partly because she was still free to refuse if she disliked the man, even though she had already refused three other men. Many marriages are still arranged in Japan, but it is illegal to exercise undue pressure. Unfortunately, the following day her mother let slip her deceit. In fact the young man had been found for her by a paid *nakodo*, an idea repugnant to Misako's spirit of independence. But after a stormy and tearful night, her mother persuaded Misako to meet Haruo Sato. They liked each other and were married six months later.

Haruo Sato, aged thirty, had a good job with an engineering company in Tokyo. Haruo and Misako live one and a half hours' commuting distance from his office, in an area where apartment rents were low enough for a young salary man's modest pay. Misako had to be a careful housekeeper, particularly as her husband would not allow her to work. He also came from a conservative family and in everything he was heavily influenced by what his company colleagues might think. Their daily routine was simple. Unfortunately for Misako, who liked a western breakfast, her husband insisted on his morning rice and *miso* soup. The preparation of this meant that she must get up at six, half an hour earlier than her husband. He was up and out of the apartment by seven. His office had a canteen so, unlike many housewives, Misako did not have to prepare a lunch-box.

She did, however, have one other morning duty. Misako was in charge of the family finances and each month her husband gave her his whole salary. She returned sufficient pocket money for his daily expenses and minor pleasures such as cigarettes and the evening drinks with colleagues. So each morning she checked his wallet and topped it up to the agreed 15,000 yen (approx. £45) he liked to carry. Larger purchases were a matter for joint consultation and often had to be postponed until the New Year or summer bonus was paid. In a good year this could equal as much as four months' salary but in a bad year it was worryingly small.

When we join the Satos, they have been married two years and

Misako is expecting her first baby in two months. Until now her days have been lonely. Her husband seldom returns home until nine o'clock and frequently later. Socialising with colleagues is an important part of working life and she accepts that, even when he returns home rather drunk from an office party. Mostly she spends the day in their small apartment, cleaning, washing, cooking, reading her choice from among the myriad of women's magazines which exercise enormous influence and selling power, and she writes a few letters to friends. She goes out shopping each day locally but tries to avoid the expensive temptations of central Tokyo. She is more fortunate than many young wives from the provinces as she made some good friends while working in Tokyo. Many young wives who move from their home towns know nobody and even making friends with your neighbours is not always easy in Japan.

Misako is not discontented. Haruo is patient and kind and on Sundays they go out together, to a concert or a movie and some cheap restaurant. He is tired when he comes home, but makes an effort to talk over supper and inquire about her day. She is still nervous about her cooking and he makes no comment since praise and encouragement are not the Japanese way.

When they married she was totally ignorant about sex, but she accepted his advances as her duty. She told him to make sure that they did not have a baby until she was ready, and on the weekly occasion he had sex with her, he wore a condom. The pill and other devices are hardly used in Japan. They say that the abortion doctors, anxious for their lucrative trade, launched a successful campaign to discredit the pill. Misako was now used to what her mother once referred to as 'the night problem'. Those three words were the only sex education that Misako received at home. She was grateful to Haruo for being gentle but found no pleasure for herself, not least because Haruo seemed to perform in isolation.

Misako often compared her life with some of her married friends. She thought of poor Junko, married to a young doctor working in one of the big university hospitals. He came from an extremely traditional family and, being the elder son, had been brought up in a very conservative way and thoroughly spoilt by his mother. He hardly spoke to Junko during their honeymoon, and had spoken very little to her since then. He was obsessed with his career and worked hard. When he came home, if he came home, he ate supper in silence and went to bed. On Sundays he slept late and for the rest of the day flopped in front of the television. Once, after many complaints by Junko, he agreed to take her away for the weekend. After the first hour on the train he started considering ways of getting home early, grumbling that the outing was interfering with his work and his chances of promotion.

Then Misako thought of dear Yuki, her closest friend at Senior High School. Yuki had been married for four years to Shige, who taught English at a school in a rough area of Osaka. It had been a love match from the start. Yuki had shyly told her that she and Shige often made love together and that although he worked hard, he always tried to hurry home to be with her. Yuki worked in an office which enabled them to save money. Every other year they had a summer holiday abroad, going by themselves to surprisingly out-of-the-way places. They represented a new generation; a romantic marriage, a closely shared life, a growing independence and a wider view of the outside world. Misako envied them and knew that the number of such young people was growing. Unfortunately, Haruo did not like foreign travel. He didn't even care for spaghetti which was Misako's favourite dish.

Now Misako has the arrival of her baby to think about. Haruo had been pleased when she agreed to have a child and she had become pregnant quickly. She was relieved as she had heard of many couples who had had difficulties in starting a family. This surprised her as Japanese tend to take their ability to have children for granted. Her husband's company arranged for her to attend a good hospital regularly while her mother offered miscellaneous advice over the telephone. Her mother-in-law had stayed for a week to help with the purchase of baby clothes and equipment. Secretly, Misako hoped for a girl who would be better company for her. But she knew that her husband and his family wanted a boy to protect the family name.

Her mother-in-law tried to make her wrap her pregnant stomach in the traditional binding cloth, and also pressed her to visit a suitable shrine to pray for a safe delivery, but Misako resisted these old-fashioned ways. She had two friends who would not enter a shrine during their monthly period from the old belief in defilement, but such ideas are dying out. Like many young people, Haruo and Misako had no Buddhist altar or Shinto shrine in their home. But both still felt a duty to help tend the family graves. And maybe as they grew older, they might turn to more traditional attitudes.

The baby arrived safely, a boy, called Makoto after his grand-father. Misako eagerly observed the tradition of going to her own home for a month to relax with her parents. She had paid a similar visit a few months after her marriage, to show her parents that she was happy in her new life. But basically she was now a member of her husband's family. Now, on her return, it was time to arrange for Makoto's first visit to the Shinto shrine, a kind of equivalent to baptism. The baby was dressed in a beautiful kimono-robe and the priest carried out brief rites of blessing and purification. It was over in a few minutes but the occasion meant a lot to Makoto's grandmother.

Life resumed in the Tokyo apartment which soon became even more overcrowded with Makoto's toys. Already ludicrously over-furnished with the obligatory wedding suite, Makoto's arrival produced further chaos. In general the Japanese are clean, particularly in their persons, but usually they are extremely untidy. Misako immediately became a slave to her child. Makoto was always on her back or by her side and, for several months, at her breast. Though the majority of Japanese women have tiny breasts, they like to breast feed their children. Misako's patience and gentleness with Makoto is typical of Japanese mothers who are wonderful with their children. Japanese childhood is an idyllic period, usually free of tears and tantrums. In a sense small children are extremely spoilt, but the fact that they move so easily into the disciplines and responsibilities of primary school life at six, shows that a firm basic security has been established. Those early years are devoted to making the child a pliant member of Japanese society in which social attitudes become reflex actions. From babyhood the mother presses the baby's head in a tiny bow as anyone enters the room. While western children are encouraged 'to stand on their own feet', Makoto is given a deep sense of dependency, first on his mother, then to a widening circle to whom he owes respect and various degrees of obligation. Significantly, while in the west a naughty child is 'shut in' his room, an extremely naughty Japanese child is 'shut out' of the house. But far from considering running away he will scream to be let in, to rejoin the group.

You will easily recognise Makoto plodding home from elementary school. During the years from six to ten, schoolbooks must be taken home in that large red leather satchel on his back, a present from grandmother. Makoto has a sister now. Tomoko is three years younger. The average Japanese family – to give sociological exactitude – is 1.7 children, and most of the young parents I know dislike the idea of an only child, but for most people the size of their family is regulated by financial considerations.

The pattern of the Satos' life is now set. Haruo has enjoyed more or less automatic promotion and increase in salary, which has enabled them to move to a slightly larger apartment. As the children progress through their three years at Junior High School to their final three years at Senior High, the whole family's life is dominated by the 'examination hell' and the struggle to get to a good university which will be the key to a good job and future security. Misako stays up late each night preparing snacks, and trying to keep up the children's spirits and their eyes open until the work is done. It is a hard time for all the family.

Although Makoto is the son of the household and commands some respect from his sister, both have equal rights to a good education. Tomoko is the more clever and gets a place at a good national university. Makoto just makes it to a respectable private university which is a heavy expense for his parents and means that he is most unlikely to get any kind of top job when he graduates.

At this time Haruo's father dies and they all go to attend the Buddhist funeral. Generally, Japanese have a Shinto wedding and a Buddhist funeral, since from early times Shintoism allowed the Buddhists to take over the unclean business of death. Death, like many unavoidable episodes in life, can be an expensive affair. Undertakers dress the front of the house with black and white curtains and in the street is a table where mourners sign their names in a book. Each mourner leaves a contribution to the funeral expenses, though part of this, like any other formal gift, must be returned in the form of a small present, the token return removing the obligation. The mourners gather before the temporary altar in the main room where the body rests, represented by a photograph taken specially for the funeral occasion before death. The priest conducts a service, relatives and friends address the dead man and a Buddhist name is given for the after-life. Rich families pay millions of yen for long memorial names, supposedly to increase status hereafter.

At the crematorium, Makoto and his father are eventually confronted with the ashes from which, using two pairs of special chopsticks, they pick out and place in a funeral urn what are considered the most vital remaining bones of the dead man. A variety of small bones are necessary to represent the different parts of his body, but most revered is the Adam's-apple, since that bone is shaped like the seated Buddha. The urn is sealed, and in due course placed in the family tomb. A succession of memorial services will be held, at first frequently but continuing, if the family remember, for fifty years.

The Buddhist funeral produces some strange results. Each year Japanese newspapers report that hundreds of funeral urns turn up among the lost property left on trains. And please note: never stick your chopsticks standing upright in a bowl of food, particularly rice. Such is the position for the chopsticks of the dead, and therefore an uncomfortable sight for any Japanese. Nor, because of the bone-choosing ceremony, should you ever try to pass food from chopsticks to chopsticks. The deeper etiquette of others' culture can be so confusing.

5

The Road to Ise

We have reached the centre of Japan but we must continue on a meandering route, picking our way between various places of interest until the road leads south to the Shinto Grand Shrines at Ise. In this mountainous area most of the plains are along the coast. Nagoya is the major city, fourth largest in Japan and most important industrial centre after Tokyo and Osaka. It has long been a centre of the ceramic industry, famous for Seto wares. Nagoya has few relics of interest and the impressive castle was, in fact, rebuilt after the Second World War. Nearby is an open-air museum at Meiji Mura, opened in 1965. The collection of Meiji and Taisho buildings includes the façade of Frank Lloyd Wright's Imperial Hotel; it survived the 1923 Tokyo earthquake, proving the claims he had made for his structure.

I had an unusual experience in Toyama, a town on the Japan Sea, famous for its delicious fish, particularly in the autumn, when I was lucky enough to make my visit. It will certainly be the only time in my life when I find myself guest of honour of a Japanese town. The fine views of the Japan Alps were obliterated by torrential rain but I learned that the town's fortune was founded by a seventeenth-century lord who encouraged the production of an early patent medicine. Its popularity spread as far as Korea and China and today a pharmaceutical industry thrives in Toyama. My business focused on a large private girls' school, owned and run by the domineering wife of a local doctor. The school taught various subjects, including dress design and dressmaking.

At that time I was establishing a craft college in the south of England, and through my contacts we were receiving a few

9 The simple moss garden in front of Chotokuin, Kyoto

NATURE AND ARCHITECTURE

10 In the author's Kyoto house the screens slide back to join the room
with the garden

11 The surrounding moat and elegant turrets of Tokyo's Imperial Palace are all that now remain of the Shoguns' former castle

MARTIAL ARCHITECTURE

12 Complex roof patterns of Himeji Castle, the best preserved and most beautiful in Japan

groups from Japan. One of those groups came from this school, and after a successful visit the Principal invited me to visit Toyama the next time I came to Japan. I agreed to give a talk about the college and to stay a night to attend a reception. Apart from preparing my talk, I gave the visit little thought. I had underrated the ambitions of my patroness who was determined to extract the maximum publicity from my short stay.

I found myself on the platform of a large hall looking out over a vista of young female faces. They were dressed in a sailor uniform still popular for Japanese schoolgirls. They sat immobile, rigidly to attention. The Principal barked sharply at the girls who promptly sat up more rigidly. She made a brief speech, barked again, and joined her staff who sat in two depressingly solemn rows at the side of the platform. I felt lost. I like to speak informally and I could not talk to 200 girls sitting in obvious discomfort, especially as I had orders to talk for an hour. I begged my audience to relax. The only movement was 400 eyes swivelling towards the staff benches. I turned to the staff and saw a look of dismay on their faces. Clearly one did not ask the girls in this school to relax. But I felt I had to win. Politely I asked the Principal to request the girls to sit at ease. The sudden arrival of two television teams saved an impasse. The Principal did not wish any disciplinary hitch to be filmed. She gave a slightly different bark and the girls subsided into reasonable comfort. It was the first, and I hope the last, time that I have to give a lecture with two television cameras thrusting into my face, my notes, and then the slides on the screen. It made the task of trying to interest 200 Japanese schoolgirls in the obscure doings of an adult education college in West Sussex more impossible than I had feared. It was a flop, but I console myself that while they were bored, they were at least bored in comfort.

After the lecture there was a press conference. This time the Principal was taking no chances. All the questions were addressed to me. All the questions were answered by her. There followed another embarrassment. These Japanese occasions always involve a formal exchange of presents. I had not come unarmed, but I was keeping my powder dry for the evening reception. My hostess was less patient. A metre-high parcel was manhandled onto the table and I removed the wrapping. When people press gifts onto foreign visitors, they often ignore the problems of their guest's long journey home. I had already guessed, whatever it was, that it must weigh around 10 kg. As the last tissue paper fell away I was calculating the excess baggage charges. The object was monumental, and several other things besides. Before me stood a hugely robust samurai, cast in solid metal. Beyond that, he was housed in a glass case that would comfortably have fitted a stuffed penguin. The shaming thing is that if I had liked the object, somehow I would have got it home. In fact, I took an instant and violent dislike to it and found myself offering fifteen reasons why, much as I liked it, it could not travel to England. In such moments one's mind plumbs the depths of hypocrisy. It was far too good for me. The risks were too great for such an important work of art. It must surely be listed as a national treasure. We compromised on a miniature tea-ceremony set which I treasure to this day.

The Principal's husband was a charming doctor who dealt efficiently with my emerging cold and an emerged cold sore and gave me a memorable fish lunch at Toyama's best restaurant. I have only to mention the occasion to any Japanese and they squirm with envy. In the Japanese mind paradise is closely followed by Toyama's autumn fish. In the afternoon we tried to do some sightseeing but the rain obscured even the buildings across the street, let alone temple gardens and mountain views. Back at my hotel the doctor turned on the television and there on the screen was West Dean College, a camera shot of one of my lecture slides, in all its pseudo-gothic splendour.

Everything about the evening reception overwhelmed me; tiredness, my cold, the enormous lunch still undigested, alcohol, the Mayor of Toyama, speeches, a gaggle of politicians, more speeches, and more speeches. I'm no novice at this sort of thing. I was once asked to be guest of honour at a dinner in Derby where I found myself topping the bill as the thirteenth speaker. In Japan public speaking gives a rare opportunity for self-expression, not something to be dispatched in three minutes. I have sat through fifteen speeches at a Japanese wedding, more intolerable as almost identical to the fifteen speeches at the previous wedding. I marvel at the stamina and empty rhetoric of the Japanese public speaker. I marvel even more at the inexhaustible patience of the Japanese audience. There must be a secret defence. I am trying to learn how to sleep with my eyes open.

I was a failure. I think I said the right things but I compressed them into four minutes, a puny performance. Next morning, with a headaché of mixed origins, I boarded a small aeroplane and, clutching the travelling tea set, nursed my hangover and my memories of Toyama back to Tokyo.

Down the coast is the famous town of Kanazawa, often called 'Little Kyoto' because of its many temples and other historic sites. Other Japanese towns have also been given this flattering title. It is absurdly misleading. Kanazawa is a charming town but it bears about as much resemblance to Kyoto as Abingdon to Oxford or Salem to Boston. Outside of Kyoto, Nara and Kamakura, you usually have to travel long distances to see a single place or building of the first quality, perhaps supported by a few minor attractions. Seeing all the best things in Japan is therefore a time-consuming process, particularly if you want to see them at their best, usually in spring or autumn.

Kanazawa, prefectural capital of Ishikawa, was the seat of the Maeda clan, second largest in the Edo period. Today, the remains of their castle provides an unusual campus for the university. Across the road is the Kenrokuen Park, constructed in 1819 around the Maeda family mansion. It is considered to be one of the three most beautiful landscape gardens in Japan, another in Mito and the third in Okayama. Kenrokuen is the largest, the name suggesting the six elements of which it is composed: vastness, solemnity, careful planning, venerability, the coolness of running water and the beauty of its landscapes.

All this is true and the garden makes a visit to Kanazawa worthwhile. Inside the entrance, just by the famous Kotoji stone lantern is a romantic view across a wide lake to where small Japanese pavilions hang over the water. In November gardeners were wrapping the old pines in elegant coats of straw to protect them from the winter. Streams run everywhere over beds of dark pebbles and between crouching rocks and on one side there are good views over the city and away to the mountains. Near the centre of the garden is the lovely building called Seisonkaku. The garden is large and full of quiet, less kempt corners with steep banks covered in flowers, or small, rushing streams which brush the tails of the hanging willows. It is a garden for every season and must be beautiful under snow.

After the garden, the other sights of Kanazawa are little more than fringe benefits. There is a short street of rather dilapidated samurai houses. One has been turned into a small museum of *kaga-yuzen* silk dyeing, an important process first developed in Kanazawa. The town has long been famous for its fine *Kutani* porcelain, to me the most attractive of old Japanese porcelains. Modern *Kutani*, on sale everywhere, is a vulgar travesty of a great tradition. There is an old geisha quarter where one fascinating geisha house is now open as a museum and retains an extraordinary old-world atmosphere. There is also the Myoryuji Temple, former temple of the Maedas, which because of its network of hiding places, secret staircases and concealed exits, has been renamed Ninjadera, temple of the 'Invisible warriors'.

After Kenrokuen, my best memory is of a fish restaurant. Would that my friend Fumio had a better sense of direction. Fumio had read about this restaurant in her guide-book. It gave the address and said it was by a bridge over a fish shop. That sounded easy enough. In the evening we set out and soon came to the bridge. We searched the area for thirty minutes with no success. At last we found the neighbourhood police box. This was manned by a large and jovial policeman with a bristly head of hair. His assistant was weedy and silent, his uniform one size too large. The big policeman, thinking we had come at least to report a stolen car or a lost wallet, leant back in his inadequate chair, rubbed his bristly head and bellowed with laughter when we reported the loss of a fish restaurant. He didn't know of any such restaurant in his area. Fumio was extremely embarrassed and tried to leave. The big policeman put out a massive hand, bellowed again and told us to wait. He was enjoying the novelty of the challenge. He telephoned directory inquiries but drew a blank. We felt we must have got the restaurant's name wrong. He questioned Fumio again, who began to look like a serious delinquent. Her nerves prevented her from seeing that the policeman was thoroughly enjoying himself, poring over maps and thumbing through directories. Eventually, he rang police headquarters and there followed a long conversation and much head rubbing. He slammed down the receiver, rubbed harder than ever, roared with laughter and announced that he had found it. His face was saved. As for ours, we had the wrong name, we were on the wrong bridge, crossing the wrong river. Fumio didn't feel like fish that night. But next day at lunch we enjoyed the cheapest and the biggest dish of delicious raw fish I have ever eaten in Japan.

To the south-east of Kanazawa, in the neighbouring prefecture of Gifu, is the pleasant small town of Takayama. How did you guess? Yes, it is also often called 'Little Kyoto'. But it is worth a visit both for some individual buildings and for its general historic atmosphere. It has been partly spoilt by tourism, but now what place in the world that boasts half an old building and a public lavatory has not? Beyond the rather drab area around the station Takayama has two complete streets of splendid old houses, a number now museums, others shops or coffee shops, though the houses are all carefully preserved. In other places there are a few fine individual buildings, most notably the Takayama Jinya, the town's huge old rice-store. Like the houses, it is of massive wooden construction, the carpentry beautiful in its functional simplicity and its grand scale. For rural buildings, do not miss Hida Minzoku-Mura, an open-air museum just outside the town (Plate 1). A variety of farmhouses and associated buildings, characterised by their high, steep, thatched roofs, are cleverly landscaped around ponds and paddocks, the museum site running up the hillside with the mountains behind. The buildings are interesting and charming and the whole museum is delightful. Allow at least two hours. We had a crisp, golden autumn morning there and I know of no more attractive folk museum in Japan.

On this trip I had Ikuyo with me. I had asked her to avoid hotels as I wanted to try a Japanese type of accommodation called *minshuku* – a rural equivalent to Britain's bed and breakfast – where, originally, Japanese farmers, with space to spare, took in a few guests giving them supper, accommodation and breakfast for a low inclusive charge. This genuine type of *minshuku* is now not so easy to find as the idea has caught on and been commercialised so that many *minshuku* are now just cheap Japanese inns with no family or rural atmosphere. It's a matter of luck, not least as the *minshuku* guides give no description of each establishment. I have stayed at several and only about a quarter of them have been the genuine article.

At the end of a long day's sightseeing we took a taxi to the Minshuku Noda, where Ikuyo had booked by telephone. After losing the way once amongst the darkening fields, the taxi dropped us off in front of a large and ramshackle farmhouse set in acres of vegetables. Inside it was warm and the farmer's wife showed us to our rooms and brought us tea, saying that supper would be at seven. My room had a tatami-matted floor and a large oil stove. These remain Japan's most popular and cheapest form of heating. A more devilish device is the *kotatsu*. A low-powered electric heater is screwed beneath a small, low table which is covered with a large quilt. Sitting on the floor, you thrust your legs under the table and tuck the quilt round your waist. It is just better than nothing, but you are a prisoner of the table and the warmth enjoyed by your legs does little but emphasise the coldness elsewhere and the growing stiffness in your back.

At seven we went downstairs where a table laid for two was set in the corner of a large room. Our hostess had a delightful rosy-apple face, permanently illuminated by one huge glittering gold tooth. We ordered beer and began a large and excellent meal of raw fish, bean-paste soup, fried bean curd, a variety of vegetables, some cooked fish, a chicken dish, all topped off with pickles and rice. During the meal the farmer came in. I asked him to join us for some beer and soon both he and his wife were sitting with us.

At first the farmer was morose and I suspected that he had already been drinking. We began talking of young people in Japan. It was obvious the farmer thought little of them. He had been brought up during the Second World War, and this seemed to have left him with a deep sense of deprivation.

'I never had a school outing,' he grumbled, rather aggressively. He downed his beer and waved to his wife to bring another bottle. He returned to this favourite theme regularly throughout the evening.

I asked his wife if there was still someone in the kitchen. She said that her elder son was clearing up. I suggested that he join us but she said he was only twenty-two and very shy. I begged her to invite him and soon he came, a gentle-faced young man in a tracksuit. Two glasses of beer eased his shyness and he told us that he was learning to cook, while his younger brother was studying engineering in Gifu. With the two men of the household seated at the table, the wife kept smiling but remained silent, (Plate 19) jumping up every now and then to fetch more beer and later to bring a bottle of whisky, by which time the evening had turned into their party.

By now the farmer had mellowed, his alcohol level having gone over the aggressive line. Even when he returned to the lost school outings, he was able to take a wider view of this calculated deprivation. Since we talked for hours I cannot remember all the ground we covered. I do recall one passage which typified his and, no doubt, many other rural people's attitude to life.

'Noda-san, do you think Japan is changing much?'

'Yes, a great deal.'

'In what way? Good or bad?'

'Bad! It's young people and the family. Parents are too soft.'

'Are you worried about this?'

'No. It does not affect me.'

Whatever the subject of discussion – Japanese politics, the oil crisis, trade friction, juvenile delinquency – as with many farmers around the world, it was always the same narrow, cabbage-patch point of view. It did not affect him. It was an interesting evening and I did not even resent my slight headache the following morning as a totally sober farmer proudly showed me his cabbages and those long, white Japanese radish which are unkindly invoked to describe Japanese girls with ungainly legs.

Heading south, we come to the large town of Gifu, capital of Gifu prefecture, and long-time producer of hand-made paper, which in turn led to the making of paper lanterns and umbrellas. It is also famous for making fireworks which are shown off each summer in a magnificent display by the central river. The town has a castle high on a hill with fine surrounding views which must have been spectacular before the urban sprawl leaked into these long valleys. This has become the story of Japan. The more I travel, the more certain I become that there is a central committee in Tokyo, chaired by some fiendish Japanese Peter Sellers character, hell bent on destroying the landscape of Japan. Their only fear is that some canny local planning committee might put three factories all in one valley, leaving the two adjacent ones unspoilt. Travel by train from Tokyo to Osaka, or Tokyo to anywhere, and you will soon realise that I am hardly fantasising.

I have experienced great kindness in Gifu and therefore have warm feelings about the town. I last went to see the summer fireworks. I looked forward to this since fireworks are so much a part of the Japanese summer, from children's maple-sparklers lit on the riverbank to the sky-fantasies of the big summer festivals. The Japanese make the best fireworks in the world but those at Gifu were beyond my most colourful expectations, perhaps because I had not seen a big fireworks display for many years. These fireworks were of the space age, each rocket diffusing clouds of scintillating stars that hung brilliantly in the dark sky. Then, with equal drama, down came the rain, sudden and torrential as only summer rain can be, the mountains around echoing to deep rolls of thunder. On the river below the lights of the cormorant boats were swallowed up in sheets of water, the hotel terrace was a swamp, and the Gifu fireworks display was over. But the few minutes when the exploding lights and fragmenting stars of the rockets clashed against the first thunder and crack of lightning was memorable.

Our hosts were deeply apologetic. My son and daughter and I, stunned by the magic of what we had seen, and less expectant than the locals, presumed that the display had defeated the rain. It was not so. Evidently, and amazingly, what we had seen was merely the introduction to the main display. I still find that hard to believe, and I hope that another summer I may see the whole show. It was only sad that our hosts were so disappointed.

Now we travel south again to Mie prefecture and a large peninsula that juts south into the Pacific, famous for historic places, Matsusaka beef, national parks and, in one of them, almost my favourite place in Japan, the ancient and sacred Shinto shrine of the Imperial family. Ise-Shima National Park lies on the eastern promontory of the peninsula, the Grand Shrines of Ise in the northern part of the park.

The shrines of Ise are still closely associated with the Imperial household. The first time I went there, police suddenly swept us out of the way of a cavalcade of black limousines full of elderly gentlemen in morning dress. We were told that these were Imperial messengers making a statutory visit. The idea of Imperial messengers in large modern cars was very appealing.

On my last visit I was lucky enough to see a more charming and more genuine Imperial messenger. We were walking up the wide, quiet avenue towards the inner shrine when a flutter of white caught my eye. We stood aside as eight Shinto priests, their black-lacquered ceremonial hats in perfect contrast to their immaculate white flowing robes, kept well clear of the ground by high black-lacquered sandals, escorted Princess Chichibu, the Emperor's sister-in-law, into the shrine enclosure where she had some official duty to perform. The solemn occasion did not prevent her from giving the crowd along the way some charming smiles.

Ise is impressively beautiful and the architecture of the shrines extremely interesting. Leaving the car park one crosses a long wooden bridge over a wide, bright river. Within the shrine park are a variety of shrines and shrine offices, but the centre of interest is the inner shrine. My only criticism of Ise, perhaps a strange one, is that if anything it is too neatly kept. The paths are swept, each shrub clipped, the flowers exactly ordered, so that only the avenue of towering cedars remain wholly in touch with nature, beyond the reach of gardener or garden design. They create the hallowed atmosphere. At a break in the trees people purified themselves in the river water before proceeding to the shrine. By now the park is left behind. The path narrows between the huge tree trunks and one feels in the forest of the gods as one approaches a flight of stone steps which lead to the wooden fence which protects the mystery and hallowed ground of Ise's inner shrine. Here the pilgrims pray, the tourist cranes his neck to catch a glimpse of the mysterious buildings, and when both are satisfied they return the way they have come. The experience is quiet and undramatic. But it is always memorable for it is a special place.

The inner shrine is said to date from the third century AD. It enshrines the Sun Goddess, mythical ancestress of the Imperial family. She was represented in the shrine by a sacred mirror, a sword and a jewel, the regalia of the Imperial family. What the shrine holds today few know, as few except the Emperor may enter. This shrine must be rebuilt every twenty-one years, a renewal ritual common to many religions. The last new shrine was built in 1973. Within the sacred enclosure are two adjacent sites, used in turn. Qualified carpenters must be kept trained for this special work, just as there are other craftsmen in Japan who continue to supply special new equipment as everything must be renewed. But everything must be identical to what went before from the building down to an elaborate set of special combs. It is believed that the simple design of the inner shrine goes back unchanged to at least the seventh century, based originally on prehistoric storehouses and granaries. Built of plain cypress wood, the style of architecture may not be used for any other Shinto shrine.

Moving from the truly sublime to the somewhat ridiculous, near to Ise is the small town of Toba, overlooking a beautiful bay rather Mediterranean in feeling, with a reddish rocky shore surrounding the glimmering sea. On a small island Kokichi Mikimoto developed the cultured pearl after years of research and failure. There is an interesting museum and hourly demonstrations by the famous women pearl-divers. It ought to be fascinating but in reality is somehow spoilt by over-commercialisation.

Just north of Toba is a simpler kind of Shinto shrine. Along the craggy shore a path leads to the view of two large rocks jutting out of the sea, symbolising Izanagi and Izanami, the creators of Japan according to mythology. The rocks are joined by a thick rope of plaited rice straw which is renewed with ceremony on 5 January each year. It is said that occasionally at sunrise Mt Fuji can be seen from this place. I always like these shrines made out of natural features. They are closer to the heart of Shinto than elaborate architecture. The spirit of Ise lives not in the shrine, but in its forest of giant cedars.

Of all Japanese institutions, Shinto is one of the hardest to explain. This is partly because historical Shinto has had so many faces and been linked with various other religions. Also, in modern Japan, Shinto seems to mean something different to each Japanese. Shinto is Japan's indigenous religion and at various times has been the nation's official religion. It was disestablished in 1945, largely because of its association with pre-war nationalism. But in various ways it has remained at the heart of Japanese culture and still plays a limited role in daily life.

The word 'Shinto' is written with two Chinese characters, *shin* meaning 'divinity' or 'god', the *to* meaning 'way'. It is often translated as 'the way of the gods'. At its most primitive it must have been a simple nature worship. Even today popular Shintoism retains strong elements of pantheism. There are the named gods who are the mythological Imperial ancestors, but each shrine has associations with a particular animal, a fox or a boar for example, while each tree may house a spirit. For centuries the life of the shrines and their various festivals have been linked with the seasons, and the cycle of agricultural life, centring on the cultivation of rice. For this reason this urbanisation of Japan in the last hundred years has separated Shinto from most people's lives.

The history of Shinto is complex as it encompasses a simple folk religion and, at certain moments in history, attempts to formulate it into a moral theology. Also at various times, from its early associations with shamanistic practices, Shinto has, sometimes under coercion, been intermingled with Buddhism, Confucianism, Taoism, and with various new religions of the late nineteenth century, such as Tenrikyo. This led to a variety of Shinto sects. It is simplest to divide Shinto into three general categories. State Shinto came and went according to official attitudes at different times. The intellectual Shinto made various attempts to elevate the religion to higher planes. Popular Shinto sustained the ordinary people over the centuries. In its own way, now mainly cultural, it continues to do so. The neighbourhood shrine is a centre of life, while the Buddhist temple is largely the centre of death.

Regrettably, Shinto is still used as a rallying point for nationalism. The pre-war military government openly identified Shinto with Japan's nationalistic ambitions and used it for their propaganda. Today's left-wing have not forgotten this. Each August the Japanese press vigorously debate whether or not the Prime Minister and members of the Cabinet are allowed under Japan's constitution to make an 'official' visit to pay their respects to the war dead enshrined at Yasukuni Shrine in Tokyo. For several years Prime Ministers have visited the shrine and signed the book in various cryptic ways which allow them to claim that their visit was a private one. The present Prime Minister, Yasuhiro Nakasone, who is given to making statements with slightly nationalistic overtones, has stirred up this annual controversy even more. The affair has now become largely a media charade.

There is a slight danger of a revival of the worst kind of nationalism in Japan, but a clear distinction should be made between patriotism and nationalism. It seems reasonable that the Japanese head of state should once a year pay official respect to the nation's war dead, the vast majority of whom were the innocent victims of their own government and many of whom suffered terribly at the hands of their own commanders. It might simplify the situation if Japan set up its own tomb of an unknown warrior, free of political or sectarian memories and interests.

Japan is a land of festivals and most of them are Shinto, springing from indigenous fertility cults, rice-growing rites and former supplications for deliverance from flood and plague. Buddhism has its festivals, but most of these are celebrated in the temples, whereas the biggest Shinto festivals take place in the street. Kyoto abounds with festivals, nearly one for each day of the year, and on some days more than one. The great Gion festival in July, for example, takes over the centre of Kyoto for four days and nights. Other festivals are small ceremonies where you can decently dispose of worn-out personal possessions such as combs and needles at a particular shrine.

Visiting a shrine on an ordinary day, however fine the buildings or beautiful the setting, there is a deserted feeling, like an empty theatre. Shrines must be visited at festival times. For a day or more they come alive and play a central role in the life of their neighbourhood. At any time you may see a few visitors, sightseers, those who have come for a special blessing or simply to make a votive offering (Plate 14), clapping their hands and bowing to the inner shrine as they make their request to the gods (Plate 15). Ownership of the shrines is hereditary. The priest and his family live in a house adjoining the shrine. Some shrines are large and wealthy, others decrepit and poor. It is amazing how so many thousands of shrines manage to survive. In the village or urban area each family is affiliated to one shrine where they may give volunteer labour, and they will make some offering during the year, even if it is only the few yen they toss into the huge offertory box at New Year.

New Year is the best time to visit a Shinto shrine. Most Japanese like to make a 'first visit' during the New Year holiday, women and children often in bright kimono and even a few men in traditional dress. The approaches to the larger shrines are lined with stalls selling trinkets, cheap toys and a variety of delicious snacks from fried squid to candy floss. Each shrine has its own shop selling devotional souvenirs, decorated arrows, plaques with the animal of the year and amulets offering protection against fire, traffic accidents and other hazards. These are colourful, happy and lively occasions, touching the heart of Japanese life.

I have often asked younger Japanese friends why they visit shrines. Most of them have no positive belief, but they would feel that something had been left undone if they stayed away. Observing the ritual is important to the Japanese, even when the meaning it once symbolised has largely disappeared. Much of the praying at shrines is now a kind of social ritual, or even a bit of fun, like consulting the fortune-tellers often found in the shrine precincts. Just as it is pleasant to be told that a handsome dark stranger is on the way, there is no harm in praying for one. Few of us really believe in the birthday cake wish, but most of us make it. There are, of course, devout Shintoists. I have seen elderly women deep in prayer before some shrine, clearly aware of a divine presence. Such devotion is probably commoner in country districts.

With its roots deeply in Japan's agricultural and rural way of life, and basically a folk religion of simple nature worship, Shinto has had a strong influence on the Japanese attitude to nature, though exactly what that has become in these modern times is not easy to say. The Japanese attitude to nature is mixed and deceptive. Foreigners immediately tend to think of such things as the exquisite gardens, the sensitive flower arrangements and the respect for natural materials such as wood and clay which Japanese craftsmen use so naturally. Japan has lived close to nature, drawn its admired materials from nature and developed a certain fine taste rooted in these relationships. But to assume that this delicate aesthetic sense is to be found in the majority of

Japanese is as absurd as expecting the whole of the Dutch nation to share Rembrandt's penetrating vision. Our idea of Japan is so largely drawn from the past and based on traditional principles of taste which at any moment in history only a tiny number of Japanese understood and enjoyed. For centuries the majority of Japanese were farmers, and farmers the world over, living day to day with the elements, are neither romantic nor aesthetic in their attitudes to nature.

Certainly, the Japanese feel strongly about nature, but many of those feelings are either ritualistic, or a blind obedience to various arbiters of taste, be it famous tea-masters, heads of flower-arrangement schools or merely television personalities who have somehow established themselves as pundits. I have often visited temple gardens or recognised beauty spots with Japanese friends, and as we stroll around I see some plants perfectly sited by an old tree. Something like the following always ensues:

'Oh, do look. Isn't that beautiful?'

'Excuse me. What?'

'Oh, those blue irises growing by that old tree.'

There is now a pause while Akiko, or Junko, or Sawako, or Tomoko thumb frantically through the pages of their official guide where, to their dismay, they find no recommendation to admire some irises by an old tree. There follows something of a 'cultural gap' in the conversation while we hurry on to find something that I like and which is also in the book, where we can unite again in joint admiration. In Japan nature is a serious and organised affair. The advantage of the system is that you cannot give your own bad taste away. Few Japanese have any confidence in their own taste, mostly rather wisely.

For most Japanese, distance certainly lends enchantment to the view. Real nature is better kept at a distance, or admired after it has been tamed within the confines of a garden or a vase of flowers. Japan does have a growing number of hikers, campers and mountaineers, and young people are acquiring a taste for outdoor life. Many Japanese have no desire to get involved in such a direct way. They flock in sightseeing buses to all the recognised beauty spots while the mountains immediately around Kyoto, even at weekends, are largely deserted.

However, even the most urbanised Japanese are deeply aware of the changing seasons, which influence nearly all they do. Their attitude is again often more ritualistic than realistic, their eye on the calendar rather than the actual weather. Each season is officially determined and, for example, all outdoor swimming pools are closed by 20 September at the latest, regardless of the fact that often Japan has hot weather for another month. Domestic life, food and dress all follow a strict and rather expensive seasonal round. One requires three sets of Japanese bedding, one for winter, one for summer and a third for the in-between temperatures of spring and autumn. The same cycle applies to clothes and with functional garments; a woman may have three weights of raincoat matched by three types of umbrella, including the parasol for summer. On a more positive note, the seasonal foods are a major source of pleasure to everyone in Japan and Japanese cuisine exploits them to the full.

I find little real evidence in Japan today for a spontaneous love of nature. Shinto influence has ritualised attitudes. The formation of the National Parks was a remarkable achievement, in the face of Japan's complicated landowning system. One hopes that this 20 per cent of Japan's land will continue to be protected from the enormous commercial pressures. In the last few months a small mountain has been half demolished behind my house to make a site for eleven small houses, leaving a huge scar of concrete across this section of Kyoto. Two miles up the road a landowner was caught in the process of demolishing a whole mountain. These eastern mountains have been the natural heritage and backdrop of Kyoto for a thousand years, but nobody really seems to care. It is accepted as part of the 'economic miracle', but it does not demonstrate any true love of nature.

13 Japan's oldest shrine, Izumo Taisha

SHINTO—THE WAY OF THE GODS

14 Votive offerings

15 Prayers at Kitano Shrine, Kyoto

16 The great burial ground at Koya-san

BUDDHISM—THE PILGRIMS' WAY

17 Jizo-san, protector of children 18 The ascent of Mt Haguro

6

Past Meets Present

NARA AND KYOTO

Yamato, the old name for approximately the area of Nara prefecture, might be called the birthplace of Japan. Indeed, the word is still used to describe those things purely Japanese as opposed to those influenced by China. From possibly the third to the seventh century AD the early emperors of Japan settled here, particularly in the region immediately around Nara known as the Yamato Plain. This was the pre-Buddhist period and, for purification and renewal after death, a new palace and capital was built with the enthronement of each emperor. Archaeologists are unearthing more and more remains of these early capitals and building a structure of fact around what has until recently been an area of myth and speculation.

The constant moving of capitals was costly and created administrative difficulties. In 710 the Empress-Regnant Gemmyo made Nara Japan's first permanent capital, which it remained during seven reigns until 783. By then the great Buddhist temples of Nara were threatening the independence of the Imperial Household and the capital was moved north to Kyoto. Because the early capitals were frequently moved, the modern sightseer will not find all the most important monuments of this period neatly assembled in the centre of Nara but must search some out in the Yamato Plain around Nara city. One could spend days visiting these sites out in the countryside, but for those with limited time I would suggest spending one day in Nara itself, and a day at the outlying Horyuji Temple.

The city of Nara is not one of my favourite places. It is full of great temples and works of art, but the town has an atmosphere which is as lifeless as a museum. The deer bow and nibble biscuits, the temples are swamped by tourists and the environs are laid out like a park. But the Todaiji Temple is the largest wooden building in the world; it contains the largest though largely derelict bronze Buddha in the world and, if that were not enough, behind Todaiji is undoubtedly the oldest 'museum' in the world, the Shosoin, with a collection of objects dating between 710 and 784, when they were donated to Todaiji and housed in the 'log cabin' style of storehouse still to be seen. The objects, some from China, are still perfectly preserved, now kept elsewhere and selections exhibited annually in the Nara Museum.

I recommend the architecture of Kofukuji Temple with two pagodas and a fine octagonal hall. At Toshodaiji Temple the Main Hall is one of the most perfect wooden buildings in the world with some magnificent early pieces of sculpture. There is also the Yakushiji Temple with a beautiful Buddhist Trinity in the Main Hall and a pagoda of unique design erected in 680. It appears to have six storeys but in fact has only three. It is humbling to remember, while looking at this elaborate and beautiful architecture of the seventh and eighth centuries, the state of European life at that time.

If I have reservations about Nara, my admiration for the great temple of Horyuji is unbounded. This is a fountainhead of Japanese culture and it is a miracle that so much remains. It was founded by Prince Shotoku in 607 and is the oldest existing temple in Japan with probably the oldest wooden structures in the world. Prince Shotoku's temple, built near his palace, was originally quite modest but was rebuilt late in the seventh century as a monastery. Although the layout and architecture include Japanese innovations there is a strong influence of Chinese architecture. Today Horyuji gives a clearer picture of T'ang religious architecture than anything that has survived in China. The main compound, with its hall and pagoda counterbalanced, is small but impressive and other parts of the monastery stretch away to the east. Here is a museum with a group of amazing pieces of sculpture, Buddhist art from the Asuka period. They are not only masterpieces but strange in their utter difference to anything else, not to mention the exquisite and sophisticated workmanship almost unbelievable in the seventh century. Prince Shotoku was a great patron, statesman, and compiler of Japan's first constitution; a devout Buddhist who promoted the establishment of Buddhism in Japan.

The power of these Nara temples and monasteries grew and by the end of the eighth century they were dominating the life of the city. In 784 the Emperor Kammu moved the capital to Nagaoka, south-west of Kyoto but after a few years the site was considered unsuitable and in 794 the capital of Heiankyo, today's Kyoto, was established a few miles north on a horseshoe-shaped plain, open to the south but sheltered by mountains on the other three sides. Emperor Kammu's first city was laid out on a Chinese grid-plan, still the basic layout of the city today, and Kyoto remained the capital of Japan until Emperor Meiji moved to Tokyo in 1868. Heiankyo, Miyako, Kyoto, to use some of its names, had been the capital and cultural centre of Japan for almost 1000 years and it remains one of the most historic cities in the world.

Kyoto is so many things, and different things to different people. It is now a huge and sophisticated city where a population of some 1.5 million live in an extraordinary mixed world of ancient and modern. At one end of its short subway is a huge fourteenth-century Zen Buddhist monastery with sixteen memorable Japanese gardens; at the other an ultra-modern and huge underground shopping centre. Between these two points there are some 2000 temples and shrines, countless gardens, six geisha quarters, four substantial department stores, museums round each corner, a thousand and more traditional shops to sell you everything from geisha hair ornaments to a complete range of traditional ironmongery, and computerised bus stops that flash up the number and position of the approaching buses.

I have lived in three different parts of Kyoto, which in various ways illustrate its three faces: the central area, a wealthy inner suburb, and the rural fringe on the eastern mountains. Rather than attempt a guidebook approach to this fascinating city, I thought it would reveal more about Kyoto and Japanese life if I described something of my life in these three places, each of which was so different yet so much a part of Kyoto. Unlike Nara, Kyoto is certainly no museum and to enjoy it to the full, one must live in it.

Many visitors to Kyoto must wander around the great temple complexes, observing small paths leading to gateways and gardens, a bit of washing on the line behind a venerable wall, a young monk cycling for dear life across a gravel court and other mysterious yet rather unrelated signs of activity, and wonder what exactly goes on in Buddhist temples and monasteries, so open yet so enclosed. For my first year in Kyoto I lived in Shokokuji, one of the five great imperial Zen temples of Kyoto (Plate 7). Let me hasten to add that on this occasion I was not living as a Zen monk but as the pampered guest of Priest Ogata and his mother in their sub-temple of Chotokuin. Within the grounds of these large temples the main temple buildings occupy the centre of the site and a number of semi-independent sub-temples surround the main temple. A large temple such as Daitokuji has some twenty sub-temples; I think Shokokuji has about twelve.

The sub-temples vary in size and prosperity, some owning great works of art. Most of them have a central building which accommodates a large temple and the necessary ancillary rooms, and the house of the priest's family which passes from father to elder son. There is usually at least one garden around the sub-temple and behind the garden a burial ground. The main job of Buddhism today is to bury the dead and to look after them in the hereafter by renaming them in death, conducting a number of memorial services and tending the burial ground. The fees for funerals and for holding memorial services are the main source of income, though in the large temples central funds may subsidise the upkeep of the buildings. The more fortunate temples with famous gardens make money from entrance fees. In other cases priests teach such arts as calligraphy, write books or, in one case, become a kind of Zen television star. More mundanely, some sub-temples take paying guests.

I was extremely lucky. My landlady, Mrs Ogata, considered herself retired. Her husband had died some years before, her elder son had succeeded him and her second son had a job in a Kyoto factory. When I first went to see her she apologised but said she was not taking any more long-term guests. When I returned to stay for a week a few months later, she relented and made it a condition only that I should not arrive before 7 April. That suited me perfectly and I agreed to move in on that day, exactly one week before term started at the university I was due to teach at for the coming year. The life of Chotokuin centred entirely on Mrs Ogata who, in certain respects, particularly her various sun-hats, was like a small, bird-like Edwardian aunt of mine, and in every respect a saint. I was nervous at first living in the middle of a temple, and Mrs Ogata soon sensed this.

'Please relax,' she urged me. 'This is your home.'

Mrs Ogata had what might accurately be described as a 'distinctive' command of the English language. I think she had simply picked it up from her husband who was a well-known Zen priest and spoke fluent English. Mrs Ogata had a splendid grasp of the basics and essentials but was short on the more decorative elements. Early on she had clearly decided to rise above adjectives, acquiring only two, 'pretty' and 'ugly'. This presented few difficulties once one had got onto her wavelength, but to start with conversations did have peculiar undertones. 'My son is ugly and he speaks very ugly English. You are so pretty.' She puts a finishing touch to one of the two exquisite flower arrangements she placed in my rooms twice a week. 'Please forgive my ugly flowers and this vase is very ugly. Your home must be pretty. These rooms are so ugly for you.' Her priest son spoke excellent English and the rooms were charming, but the denigration demanded by Japanese modesty, combined with Mrs Ogata's simplified English, produced some bizarre results.

The nature of my 'rooms' was the reason I could not occupy them before 7 April. The two living rooms and a small room for storage ran along the front of the temple, overlooking the impressive entrance gateway and a lovely moss-covered Zen garden designed around a very old and carefully nurtured pine tree (Plate 9). They were not strictly rooms but sections of a ceremonial corridor leading into Chotokuin's temple which was used only when the Head Priest of Shokokuji made a formal visit, a rare occasion. At other times a series of sliding screens divided the extremely wide corridor into functional rooms. A few days before my arrival had been the seventh anniversary of the death of Mrs Ogata's husband, a major anniversary in the long series of memorial services and one at which the Head Priest officiated. Normally, the memorial services that took place two or three times a week were simple affairs. A few relatives would visit the family tomb, say a few prayers with Priest Ogata and offer incense, after which they would be given refreshment in one of the small rooms beside the temple.

Life in the temple was informal. My esoteric and exotic dreams of temple life were soon exploded and replaced by experiences of cosy domestic life. The three rooms in the front did not serve all my needs and there were outposts of my little empire scattered around the extensive back area of the temple buildings which in two places enclosed charming small courtyard gardens. It took me a little time to get used to stepping out of my bedroom, in the hot weather not always very adequately dressed, straight into the handsome temple with its spread of forty-two tatami mats, centring on a high altar richly hung with glistening brocades.

At the north-east corner of these solemn precincts was my enormous refrigerator, and just beyond, carved from the corridor, the smallest kitchen in the world, one mat or roughly one metre by two metres. This was also my route to my lavatory, a choice of two bathrooms and my laundry area which looked over a waste-land of bamboos. It is a Buddhist belief that bad things come out of the north-east. Strictly speaking the waste-land was due north but out of it came two of the modern plagues. The bamboos prolifically bred the biggest, hungriest mosquitos known in nature and, beyond, the teachers in a large cramming school droned out their precious knowledge in a monotonous one-note chant from ten in the morning until midnight, or beyond. These were the only hardships of temple life.

Mrs Ogata came from Kyushu, Japan's southern island. They say that people from Kyushu are particularly warm-hearted. Mrs Ogata combined the warmest of hearts with a splendid Japanese pragmatism. For her, life was for living, including life in her temple. After I had been in Kyoto for only two days I realised that I must have transport and that a bicycle would be ideal. That sounds simple enough but being tall I had a long hunt to find a second-hand bike with a large frame and large wheels. Eventually I tracked down a splendid green monster, touched here and there with rust, but strong and roadworthy. It had no gears but Kyoto has few serious hills. For some reason I could not return to Chotokuin with my new acquisition until rather late and I did not like to disturb Mrs Ogata while she was cooking supper to ask her to show me some corner in her yard where I could keep my serviceable but unquestionably (even in Mrs Ogata's English) ugly machine. Somewhat shamefacedly I left it leaning outside my rooms, even in the dusk its hideousness dominating the delicacy of the Zen garden.

The following morning my alarm clock went off at six o'clock. Although an alarm of almost unfailing punctuality, it was not a mechanical device but the gentle whisper of Mrs Ogata's garden broom sweeping the moss in the front garden. Goodness, I thought, the bike. I shot out of bed and eased back the sliding doors. Mrs Ogata looked up from her sweeping with a smile and a good morning.

'Mrs Ogata, I am so sorry about the bicycle. I got back late last night and didn't like to disturb you.'

'What bicycle?' asked Mrs Ogata, peering round her.

'This hideous machine. I am so sorry. If you could just show me some corner at the back, I can easily keep it there.'

'Ah so. Why don't you leave it there.'

'I can't possibly leave it here. I mean it's hideous and it ruins your beautiful garden. I can't leave it here.'

'Why not? It is more convenient for you.'

The rusty old bicycle remained there. There is no arguing with a woman from Kyushu. Even worse, in the autumn it was joined by my son's bike. Mrs Ogata honoured him with a tiny set of rooms right alongside the High Altar. These days, as I wander around the great temples of Kyoto, I feel very much at home. The smell of incense mingles with the smell of cooking and the chanting of the sutras is quickly followed by the baseball results on TV. Those imposing façades and wooden gateways conjure up many memories. I shall never forget Chotokuin, because I can never forget Mrs Ogata.

At the end of my first year, the university suddenly asked me to stay a second year, but it was not possible to remain at the temple. I went house hunting with one of my kind students and, after one false start, found a small, modern apartment in one of Kyoto's most attractive residential areas, by the east bank of the Kamo-gawa River. It was different in every respect from Chotokuin, a sudden jump from a seventeenth-century temple to a newly built 'mansion', the snob name that Japanese apply to the more expensive apartment blocks. Their social desirability is further emphasised with a variety of absurd names borrowed equally from old Europe or new California. I was in residence at 'Kamo Heights' but might just as well have found myself in the 'Chateau Kamo' or 'Kamo Villas'. What's in a name you may ask? A great deal in this land of the logo.

The temple had been on the northern side of the Imperial Palace, within the heart of the city, surrounded by huge, noisy avenues and without one breeze from June through to early September. Shimogamo, my new area, was on the northern edge of the city centre, a wholly residential area, rich, traditional and cooler. Shimogamo is a network of small streets and lanes lined by houses owned for generations by the occupying family. There are very few apartment blocks, even small ones like mine. The area has been sadly modernised in the last twenty years. Coming home in a taxi one day, after I had given the driver my address, he asked me if I knew that only fifteen or twenty years ago the streets just south of my apartment had been so traditional in appearance that samurai movies had often been made there. I could hardly believe him as the area had such a modern look to me. The next day I walked around the neighbourhood and for the first time realised how many old houses filled the streets. In many cases dreadful modern façades had been imposed and the age and original character of the house could be gauged only by looking at the unmodernised sides. In many cases the effect had been ruined simply by a high concrete wall erected across the front. There were still some beautiful old wooden houses, a few with large gardens, but the overall face of the neighbourhood had been sadly desecrated in an absurd scramble to keep up with the times, a scramble that will eventually ruin Kyoto.

My own apartment block was, I am afraid, an example of the greatest threat to the Kyoto environment, the rising roofline of the city which is slowly shutting out the view of the surrounding mountains. I think my landlady's family must have owned a large house on that corner which had been demolished to make way for a block that included a large house for her family and twelve small but pleasant modern apartments. Both land and building are desperately expensive in central Kyoto. This forces people to get the maximum return on their investment, which usually means pushing up the building to the maximum height allowed by the regulations, or maybe higher if you know the palm to grease. The central block of Kamo Haitsu had a third storey which towered above the surrounding residential area. The neighbours were so upset that my landlady made her apology by keeping those two apartments empty for two years, by which time a number of neighbouring buildings had overtaken hers. I was the first tenant in one of those upper apartments. To summarise the problem: when I moved in, my living room enjoyed a superb southern view across to the mountain of Daimonji, while from my balcony at the back I could see the whole arc of the northern city. When I left five years later, new high buildings had diminished my southern view by 40 per cent and my northern view by 25 per cent – all in five years.

At one end of our block, and running parallel with the river was what I call Kyoto's 'millionaires' row', the large houses of wealthy industrialists and others who enjoyed a view over the river. Some of the houses were exquisitely built in traditional style with lovely gardens. Others were expensive but unimaginative essays in modern architecture, some inappropriately topped off with plastic wrought iron and reproduction Greek sculpture.

The house immediately opposite me, which I overlooked, belonged to a family associated with the kimono trade. In Japan you must play your role and therefore people in traditional trades and crafts should live in traditional-style houses. While I was there they demolished their old house and built a new and larger one, a year-long process which taught me in the greatest detail the traditional building processes. Before anything else, all the precious trees from their small garden, and the better rocks were uprooted, wrapped with extreme care and carried away to some safe place. Once the site was cleared, Shinto priests came to mark out and bless the spot and then with great speed very skimpy foundations were laid and the whole frame went up in two days. A lorry arrived with every piece pre-cut and numbered and about six nimble-footed carpenters put the huge jigsaw together until the last rafter and roof plank was in place. I have never seen a more neatly organised piece of work in which not even one nail was dropped from start to finish. The completion of the frame is the 'topping out' for a Japanese house and a party followed at which large quantities of beer were consumed.

I loved the neighbourhood of Shimogamo. Although firmly locked into metropolitan Kyoto, it had the life and atmosphere of a village and centuries ago, no doubt, that was what it had been, clustering around the southern shrine of Shimogamo which was founded long before Kyoto. Today it has sprawled north in a maze of narrow streets full of flowers, shaded by huge trees in the neighbouring gardens, and everywhere children playing everything from hop-scotch to baseball. Elderly residents gossiped on the street corners, mothers wheeled their infants to the neighbouring playground, the vans collecting newspapers and cardboard fought a running war for trade through their tiresome loudspeakers. The butch, unshaven driver at the wheel hardly fitted the female syrup-sweet voice on the never-ending tape. Early in the morning about once a week we were woken by two ragged-robed Zen monks with begging bowls and hoarse cries, at night the pipes of the noodle van, and throughout the long, hot summer an orchestra of cicadas in the huge camphor tree opposite.

Many Japanese are shy of foreigners, not without good reason. Their life follows an orderly pattern supported by a thousand rules of etiquette, respect language and a confusion of social traditions beyond the foreigner's grasp. However well meaning, however keen to belong, he or she will inevitably fail to observe the ground rules and create embarrassment, particularly for those Japanese with no experience of foreigners. I was fortunate in having a kind and tolerant landlady and in time I got to know one or two of my neighbours. Neighbourliness is important in Japan and when you move into a new neighbourhood, you may give each of your near neighbours a token present of good will, a trifle like a box of sugar. Present giving itself is ringed with pitfalls so whenever possible I play safe and aim my presents at the children in the family. All Japanese adore their children and a gift to a child is less of an obligation to the parents.

I was lucky to make friends with a young couple living on the ground floor with their shy little daughter, Mami-chan. It was a chance meeting. I arrived home rather late one night and went to the communal post box to see if I had any mail. There was already a man standing there and as I came up he turned and said in most excellent English, 'Aren't you the famous professor from London?' It was a flattering but wholly inaccurate description, but it led to a warm and most rewarding friendship. Masaoki was a lecturer in physics at Kyoto University and devoted most of his long hours to research into polymer structure. He was extremely clever and his English was surprisingly good, particularly as he had left Japan only once.

Masaoki had lived in Shimogamo all his life, in an old house nearer the Shimogamo shrine. Although he was only about thirty-four, he had seen many changes in the area and his parents had told him of life there long before the Second World War. Apart from the continual modernisation and rebuilding of houses, the reconstruction of the Kamogawa river, which is the western boundary of the area, must have changed its character. At certain times of the year in Kyoto there is torrential rain and in the old days the river often flooded. Eventually throughout this area the banks of the river were reconstructed, the water level controlled and huge storm drains installed.

Today the river banks have the look of a municipal park as concrete edgings and unwanted flower beds proliferate. Before the river was reconstructed, it must have been more natural in appearance though the floods were clearly both damaging and dangerous. I once had a suitably humbling experience on the river bank, where I walked incessantly as it was a place of infinite pleasures and changing views. One September morning I woke very early and realised that I had never seen the sunrise. I dressed quickly by the first light of the dawn and hurried to the river bank from where I could look to the eastern mountains. There, in great bright yellow-golden splendour, the sun was rising behind the dark peak of Mt Hiei, Kyoto's highest mountain. It was early in the morning and I was most surprised to see so many people about, strollers with their dogs, track-suited joggers and a few fishermen preparing for an early cast. What surprised me even more in this city, famed for its social reserve, was that everyone I passed gave me a little bow and a warm good morning. Usually I could walk for six miles along the river with not one passer-by acknowledging my existence.

Walking thoughtfully home I soon had it all worked out in terms of Japanese group-psychology. Obviously, all those who got up so early to exercise by the river, by their special effort, formed a temporary 'group' who were able to acknowledge other members of this group. Delighted with my expert analysis of this small piece of the Japanese social scene, I arrived home and picked the newspaper up off the floor. A headline on the front page caught my eye. A simpler explanation was revealed. It was a public holiday: Respect for the Aged Day.

Such experiences are suitably humbling. Without doubt, in 'the village' I was something of the local 'joke' if not exactly the village idiot. I never noticed any other foreigners living in that area or shopping in our village street. Yes, we had a splendid village high street, with a covered market and many other shops, some quite sophisticated. The flower shop at all seasons presented a ravishing sight and since one needs only three flowers for a Japanese flower arrangement one could indulge in wildly out-of-season extravagances or have irises all the year around. I always enjoyed our local hardware shop, partly because of the fascinating range of their stock from lovely Japanese carpenter's tools and kitchen knives through to every modern western convenience, often made rather more convenient in Japan. It was run by a cheerful father and son. The son did not know much English but had a wonderful vocabulary of the ultimate obscurities of the hardware trade. Often, as I cycled to the shop, I would wonder how on earth I was going to explain the certain little thingumajig I required to mend the lavatory or fix a broken armchair. We would fumble around in our hybrid 'Janglish' until a light of revelation would break over his crumpled face.

'Ah so, ball-cock lever, dome-of-silence you want.'

It was exactly what I wanted, but how the devil did he know? I still go back there for household goods. I also retain the services of my Shimogamo beerman. Luckily he also thought he had to retain me, so we are both happy. In a neighbourhood like Shimogamo you can telephone for just about everything. Japan is the land of the delivery service from bedroom suites to lacquer bowls of *o-sushi*, raw fish on vinegared rice. Indeed, one of my dear neighbours, too nervous to cook for me, ordered the whole many-course meal from a famous restaurant, dishes, cutlery, glasses, the lot. But my rather Dickensian little beerman was always my favourite, a frail if wiry figure heaving twenty-bottle crates of Kirin up the stairs, always grinning, even when, a month or two ago, he appeared looking like death, heaving crates three days after having had his appendix removed. I like my new neighbourhood but I'm glad that the beerman agreed to move with me.

Ever since I came to Kyoto eighteen years ago I have dreamt of having a small traditional house with a real Japanese garden. I found it a year ago except that it is more beautiful and more traditional than anything I had really hoped to find (Pl. 8 & 10). The house is on the slopes of the eastern mountains at the north-east corner of the city in a historic area called Ichijoji, until recently a farming area which had long been famous for supplying vegetables and flowers to the city. Today, old women in peasant costume still trundle carts around the neighbourhood selling the produce of the remaining fields, and in between the drab apart-ment blocks and the suburban villas vivid green rice-fields brighten the area. A month or two ago I met an executive from Japan Airlines who told me that this was his first visit to Ichijoji for exactly thirty years when he had been a student at Kyoto University. Returning that day he had been totally lost as he remembered a wholly rural area with farmhouses and a few traditional private houses set amidst the open fields running across the foot of the mountains up to the famous Imperial gardens of Shugakuin. Kyoto has changed so rapidly and con-tinues to do so.

Despite a great deal of suburbanisation, Ichijoji has kept something of its rural character, both in its people and the local buildings. Just after I moved there was an exceptionally heavy snowstorm; snow normally hardly settles in Kyoto. I went out to post a letter and I noticed that everyone up on the mountainside had strong rubber boots. In the street below the urbanites were picking their way uneasily, their smart patent-leather keeping out neither wet nor cold. Many people up here, though they have sold their land and built modern villas, are only one generation removed from farming stock. There are also still a number of lovely old farmhouses scattered to the north, some smartened up, others still shabby, their yards full of baskets, hoes, carts and maybe a small piece of farm machinery.

It is an area of lanes, sometimes country lanes with morning glory running riot over the hedgerows and steep stone steps leading up to small temples clustering against the forest edge. There are a few grand houses with large and beautiful gardens and the families may well have lived up here for centuries. The most beautiful house, which I believe belongs to the oldest local family, has an amazing pine tree from which two branches have been trained out along the top of the wall in different directions, each branch now stretching some 30 ft from the main trunk; bonsai on an enormous scale. In spring the air of Ichijoji is clouded with cherry blossom, in June the hydrangeas splash the roadsides with blue and herald the rainy season, and summer goes out on the red and white glory of the 'monkey-sliding' tree, more sedately the crape-myrtle. The area has a few major tourist attractions. There is the scholar's hermitage of Shisendo, a garden whose design is constructed of huge and carefully pruned azaleas replacing the rocks which provide the basic structure of gardens elsewhere. Its design is also a model of controlled space, the narrow entrance pathway restricting the senses in preparation for the moment when one enters the main hall and looks out on an expansive stretch of raked sand and beyond to the wooded mountainside. The area around here is picturesque with the narrow, concealed entrance steps leading up to the hermitage, a shrine gateway beyond, opposite a small waterwheel, and just below a rustic pickle shop, its thatched roof bright with growing flowers. For the truly esoteric, climb the steep road into a mountain grotto where the faithful of the Shingon sect moan their prayers to the Indian-like gods set in dark rock caves and figures of *tanuki*, the folk racoon or Japanese badger, enormously endowed about his private parts, who will bring you luck or something.

A little further north, where the road winds between open fields and the neat botanical garden of a well-known pharmaceutical company, the temple of Manshuin is tucked away, pleasantly dilapidated and ignored by the crowds, but with a fine garden which plays with the two symbols of longevity, the crane represented by pine trees, and the turtle symbolised by flat rocks.

The buildings and rooms for the tea-ceremony are also important
while in the centre of the complex is a rustic courtyard garden
with a rather eccentric stone lantern and a pretty well-head.
Fortunately, there are still beautiful temples in Kyoto which have
never found favour with the bus tours.

Manshuin's history epitomises the chequered career of so
many Kyoto temples. From the founding of Kyoto, to avoid the
priestly dominance of Nara, the authorities encouraged the
building of temples, outside the city, on the mountainsides. Even
today few of the important temples are found in the city centre
and many lie several miles out within the folds of the mountains or
spread out below their feet. These precautions proved useless
and throughout the medieval period great monastic armies, particularly from Hiei in the north-east, marched down to threaten
the government and the city. This menace was finally subdued
only in the sixteenth century. Amidst all this turbulence, plus such
constant natural disasters as fire and flood, temples were wholly
or partly destroyed, and exact or fairly exact replicas were built
over and over again, but by no means always in the same place.
For example, Manshuin was founded early in the ninth century
on the slopes of Mt Hiei. Later it was moved to the far west of
Kyoto and after that to near the centre, immediately north of the
present Imperial Palace. And finally, in the seventeenth century,
it returned to near its original site, this time below the slopes of
Mt Hiei. And although the temple is revered as a ninth-century
foundation, its celebrated building dates only from about 1630.
Kyoto temple history is complicated, not least because so much of
it tends to be based on tradition rather than documentary
evidence.

I live in the garden of a large Ichijoji house, none of it older, I
think, than one hundred years, but that is old for a house in Japan.
The house was owned by a Japanese doctor who specialised in
Chinese medicine and who grew many of his herbs on his surrounding land, a cultivation that requires a government licence,
presumably because the herbs include drugs and poisons. He
died many years ago and his huge multi-drawered herb chest still

fills the entrance hall. His widow, whom the neighbourhood believe to be eighty-six, is reticent about her age. Approaching the subject in a roundabout way, I once asked how old her son was. There was an enormous pause for mature consideration. At last came the Delphic answer:

'Ah so, he is over thirty.'

The doctor, evidently, was a devotee of the tea-ceremony. The garden contains a charming rustic and thatched tea-house which must have been built with the garden, about one hundred years ago. I live in the beautiful tea-ceremony end of the garden and my small house is really a summer waiting-room for those about to attend the ceremony (Plate 10). The front door is under 3 ft high, forcing visitors to enter crouching and in this way to induce in them a suitable spirit of humility, leaving the pomp and circumstances of daily life behind to proceed along the spiritual way of tea.

Each of the places I have lived in Kyoto to some extent symbolise different aspects of this highly individual city. Chotokuin opened a gate into the rather enclosed life of Japanese Buddhism, in itself a mixture of the ritualistic and the homely. Shimogamo showed traditional family life being eroded by the waves of commercialism and materialism sweeping over Japan. Up on the mountainside Ichijoji still shows traces of an older rural life but I suspect they, too, will be swept away in another twenty years. The house in which I write, its roof too long neglected and the wooden foundations beginning to rot, may have collapsed by then. The thatch is already slipping from the old tea-house. My landlady, still fashion crazy in her eighties, thinks nothing of buying Paris dresses but deeply resents the estimate from the thatchers.

I loved all three neighbourhoods and each taught me much about Kyoto and Japan. I shall always remember returning at night to the temple, walking through the pine wood which filled its large precinct; the quietness, the tall barred gates and the long white, blind walls made it a secret place. I loved the daily bustle of our high street in Shimogamo, the woman in the chicken shop who always corrected my halting Japanese, the old saddler who

mended shoes and was so enthralled with the British workmanship of mine, the rather 'cockney' character who gutted the fish so
neatly on the fish stall and the motherly soul nearby who always
picked out the best vegetables for the 'foreigner'. And up on the
slopes of Ichijoji I have the choice of two worlds. Three minutes
down the steep hill on my bicycle the busy city stretches out, the
flashing lights of the large *pachinko* parlour reminding me that I
have dropped back into 'civilisation'; there is also the warm
welcome I always get at the local post office and the endless
fascination of our local supermarket where the range of food from
around the world increases monthly. In the other direction, three
minutes up the hill, through a small local Shinto shrine, I am on
the forested mountainside where I can walk along steep and
isolated paths for miles in each direction, the path plunging into
small folds, gorges and tiny valleys, every now and then reaching a
point where there is a break in the trees and northern Kyoto is
spread out at one's feet, a patchwork of tiled roofs, the occasional
glint of water, intruding concrete towers, clusters of dark tree-
tops, all fading into the distant shadows of the western mountains.
Wherever you stand, Kyoto takes its beauty and mood from the
mountains that surround it on the north, west and east. The
shapes and colours of the mountains are of endless variety. Mount
Hiei, the highest peak, has a different appearance from every
angle in the city, and from each position dominates the surrounding mountains in a different ways. At each season, and at each
hour of the day in each season, colours change and the light
changes. The most striking feature of these seasonal reflections
are not really the vivid greens of summer or the burning reds and
golds of autumn, but the lengthening and deepening black and
violet shadows that emphasise the complex pattern of the
mountain's contours and continually remake and remould them.

When I first came to Kyoto the view of the mountains was more
or less uninterrupted everywhere, even in the centre of town and
the relationship between the mountains and the city was the
essence of its character, with houses and the great outlying
temples folded into the foothills. Today local law freely allows

seven-storey buildings, and many go higher. As each of these buildings obscures another view of the mountains, Kyoto is destroying its character and its unique beauty.

The Buddhist priests, their black and white robes flowing, hurtle down the streets on streamlined scooters. An elegantly dressed lady purchases her exquisite tea-ceremony cakes at a shop established 200 years ago. In the Pontocho geisha quarter a girl in a pretty cotton kimono with a lemon-yellow sash folded like a huge butterfly across her back, nods to a girl in a T-shirt and sloppy blue jeans. Only the *One-san*, murmured with the nod, gives away that the girl in jeans is an off-duty geisha being greeted by her 'younger sister', a *maiko* or geisha in training. The carpenter has arrived. Down to the plumb-line and every saw, his tools come straight out of a print by Hokusai, but he did a perfect job in fitting a complicated piece of plastic guttering. In my own kitchen, along with the liquidiser and the electric coffee-machine there are many tools and dishes that the western housewife would not recognise or know how to use. Kyoto is a showcase for the bewildering mixture of traditional methods and modern fads that make up the pattern of modern Japanese life.

Most Japanese do not find it difficult to blend the traditional with the modern and the western in their lives, nor do they suffer any confusion. The reason for this is that in most Japanese people there are two distinct areas which allow two ways of life. Within the heart of each person is their Japanese life, centring on their strong sense of Japaneseness, of uniqueness, which is both a source of pride and separation, and of their duties and obligations to family, friends, firm, even to Japan itself. My friends often say 'We Japanese'. I don't think I ever use any phrase like 'We British'. The Japanese word for foreigner, *gaijin*, means literally 'outside person'. For most Japanese this inner area of belief, thinking, feeling and living is their reality and is inviolate. Personal desires that run counter to the demands and disciplines of that inner area will be considered by others as selfish, emotional, irrational. Sustaining this inner self and way of life demands sacrifices that most westerners would find intolerable. It is the antithesis of individuality. The 'pressures of society' are also burdensome to most Japanese, so society allows each person an outer area of activity where freedoms are permissible providing that they do not threaten the inner area. Some of the freedoms, mostly for men, are essentially Japanese, such as their tolerance of drunkenness, a considerable sexual licence, and a marked indifference to the dangers of smoking, this being a cheap and almost essential release. All objects from abroad, sometimes including foreigners, can exist happily in this area, many of them little more than amusing toys which bear no relation to Japanese reality.

There is a relevant Japanese proverb which says that 'when a man is away from home, he is immune from shame'. There are many instances when 'being away from home' is an alienation or separation from a man's inner area of behaviour. If a person's situation becomes too non-Japanese, their behaviour may start to match. There have been complaints from all over the world of the bad behaviour of male Japanese tourists. Nearer home, seated in their cars, in a sense a non-traditional, western context, often the Japanese driver becomes aggressive and selfish, enjoying the release that motoring gives him from everyday disciplines at home or in the office.

Nothing is harder than to identify or predict than real change in Japan. This conservative country is exceptionally resistant to change. When change does occur, it seems to happen more slowly than elsewhere. Since I first came to Japan, I have heard people say, 'There must be big changes in the next five years.' There have certainly been a lot of small changes but not many big enough to alter that inner identity of the Japanese. What does happen is that Japan, with a long tradition of borrowing and a genius for absorbing, slowly allows certain things to move from the outer to the inner area when they have incubated long enough in the outer area to be rehatched as something acceptably Japanese. Sometimes the re-styling may be superficial, making certain foods sweeter or certain fashions softer. Sometimes more fundamental things are re-styled to fit the Japanese way of life, the acceptance of so-called 'love marriages', the slow emergence of the weekend, western-style houses and furniture. These introductions and changes have had a greater influence on some people than others, particularly the young. But, in Japan, often the young radical eventually emerges as the middle-aged conservative. The ability of society and the big companies to tame their members is shown, for example, by the fact that during the serious student riots of the 1960s some companies went out of their way to recruit the most radical leaders, confident that they could harness their energy and gifts of leadership while bridling their revolutionary ideals.

Japan is changing, however slowly, and the process may accelerate slightly over the next twenty years as international trade forces Japan to become a more active member of the international community. Traditional life, in its physical forms, is already on the way out as young people move to western homes with western beds and western foods. As everywhere in the world, especially where the wife is working, whole or part time, convenience is everything. Traditional houses, bedding, gardens, food all take a great deal of work and the surest signpost to Japan's domestic future is on the shelves of the supermarkets where more and more is 'instant', be it noodles or spaghetti bolognaise.

Commercialism is also eroding traditional life. Domestic life was essentially thrifty, requiring the minimum of furniture and household equipment and a low-budget diet. Western life-styles offer an almost unending range of consumer goods, not least to the Japanese who, if they take up anything, be it cake-making or golf, must have every single piece of equipment before they feel they can get to grips with the new skill. They are besotted by clothes, equipment and gadgets which makes them a wide-open target for commercialism, advertising and the advice that pours forth from dozens of magazines each week. Commercialism has attacked traditional life from another direction. The admired arts of Japan such as the tea-ceremony, flower-arrangement, calligraphy, kimono and anything that can be taught by a recognised master, have all become mainly a matter of money, and on occasion a cause of bribery and corruption. Tradition still dictates that girls should take lessons in tea and other elegant accomplishments, one way of increasing their chances of finding a good husband. It's all extremely ritualistic as most girls take a lot of expensive lessons but few acquire any real skill. Every now and then they will be required to take a meaningless test for which there is a considerable entrance fee. They automatically receive their certificate and automatically must send their tea-master or flower-arrangement teacher another considerable sum in appreciation of the certificate.

The money involved in such activities is considerable. When the son of Japan's leading tea-master married a minor Imperial princess in 1983, the followers of that school donated a wedding present of 60 billion yen, the largest wedding present recorded in Japanese history. The government also paid the princess 90 million yen compensation for the loss of her royal rank. Japan is certainly an economic miracle for some, not least those long-established within the traditional world. The absurdity of it all can be seen in the fact that while the tea-ceremony was devised originally for the pleasure and spiritual refreshment of a tiny group of friends, today it has been vulgarised into a performance where several hundred wealthy women buy tickets to see the master perform. There are more ways than one of destroying the traditions of Japan.

The trouble is that the traditional Japanese way of life was evolved for a predominantly rural society with a three-generation family living out its life in a seasonal cycle that was relevant to both their way of life and their means of livelihood. Much of that tradition and traditional way of thinking is becoming irrelevant to modern urban life. Japan tends to try and solve new problems with old remedies but there are distinct signs that such conservative methods must sooner or later be replaced or at least adapted to new circumstances.

Kyoto has the second most prestigious national university and some twenty private universities and two-year colleges, the largest private university having over 20,000 undergraduates. That makes this chapter a suitable place for considering the educational system of Japan, an extremely topical subject since, only recently, the Prime Minister, Mr Nakasone, opened the first meeting of the educational advisory committee he has established to consider sweeping reform of Japan's educational system. While many changes are obviously needed, both at school and university level, it is only fair to add that the general standard of school education in Japan is higher than most, with many dedicated teachers and about 100 per cent literacy, despite one of the most difficult written languages in the world. There is no doubt that school education is taken seriously in Japan but it is a system of meritocracy without much provision for the gifted. Shaped for the purposes of Japanese society and based on strong group identification, classes tend to be conducted at the pace of the slowest. Without doubt the post-war educational system has served Japan well, particularly industry and commerce. But in the full humanistic meaning of the word one could argue that while the Japanese are the most literate people in the world, in certain ways they are among the worst educated.

During the post-war American occupation many changes were imposed on Japan. Most of them, including the democratic constitution, have been accepted happily but many Japanese have remained unhappy with the post-war changes in the educational system which basically brought the American school structure to Japan. Today every Japanese child must attend government-approved schools from the age of six to fifteen. The system is called 6–3–3–4, i.e. six years at elementary level from six to twelve; three years at Junior High School from twelve to fifteen; three non-compulsory years at Senior High School from fifteen to eighteen, which 85 per cent of children achieve; finally, the normal first-degree university course is four years, but there are many two-year colleges, particularly for girls.

At the other end of the scale, there are a growing number of kindergartens and nursery schools which are all now subject to

Ministry of Education regulations and some are run by the state. The state system is duplicated throughout by private schools, and there are a vast number of ancillary private cramming schools to help students over the various examination hurdles. There are even a few private boarding schools, some of which cater particularly for children who have lived abroad with their parents and who have fallen behind the Japanese curriculum. Finally, each prefecture provides schools for the disabled and handicapped all of which have dormitories for children unable to return home each night.

Since the Second World War, bitterly opposed, if not always constructively, by a strongly left-wing teachers' union, Japanese society and conservative commercial interests, in fulfilling what they saw as Japan's economic needs, have distorted the educational system. More and more the prestige of a particular university – but in no way how you perform there – dictates the job available on graduation. In certain cases, a place at Tokyo University alone may not be enough for the best civil service jobs, which also require a place in the prestigious economics or law faculty. If you examine the 'establishment' of Japan, in both government and commerce, the majority of the men at the top (there are few women anywhere near the top) have all graduated from Tokyo, Kyoto, or the most prestigious private Tokyo universities, Keio and Waseda. In a nutshell, the university that a boy of eighteen passes into from his Senior High School will dictate the pattern of the rest of his life, and few override the system.

This system, which grows more oppressive, puts terrible pressures on both parents and children. Kindergartens, private schools and cramming schools, all of which can increase the chance of passing into a good university, charge high fees, while the fees charged by the leading private universities are becoming increasingly heavy. Apart from the financial pressures, children are expected to work intolerably hard from an early age and mothers sit up late at night with their sons and daughters.

And what is the substance of all this school education and the culminating university entrance exams? Naturally, learning to read and write the Japanese language with a minimum of 2000 Chinese characters is central and takes up a good deal of the middle years. Beyond that the syllabus is wide, so crowded that some subjects including English were trimmed in 1983. Maths is well taught, but most subjects are memory exercises in which vast gobbets of information are learned without much sense of meaning or context. I once travelled by car all over France with a Japanese girl. At every major town we came to I was given some correct piece of information such as, 'Your Black Prince fought here', or 'Molière was born here', but trying to follow up these observations, each time I found they were isolated facts, memorised with no real understanding.

The final entrance exams are largely a matter of memory with the student forced to learn many pages from several novels as only a perfect knowledge of those pages will enable him to give the exact quotations demanded of him in the exam. The end result of this system, when combined with the other inhibiting strictures of Japanese society, is a nation of people who are meticulously painstaking, have unusually well-trained memories but cannot think for themselves and have noticeably inflexible minds. Perhaps that is exactly what Japanese society wants.

The reader might well suppose that having undergone such a severe regime to achieve university entrance, and the status of the university being so influential over anyone's future career, that university life and one's course of study there were the high point of Japanese education. For the most part the exact opposite is true. Getting into a good university is all that matters. For many, what you do there is of no significance. Ezra Vogel's popular work, *Japan as Number 1*, admired and praised nearly everything in modern Japan, expressing reservations only about university education. I would go further and say that describing these institutions of study as 'universities', a western word loaded with ideas of serious scholarship and intellectual inquiry and freedom, is in most cases extremely misleading.

But one must be careful of generalisations for my own experience is limited. I did teach both undergraduate and graduate students in the most prestigious department of one of Japan's oldest and best-known private universities. I have also had a number of Japanese friends who teach a variety of subjects in both national and private universities, besides even more friends who have been students at university all over Japan. From this personal knowledge I would make a few observations.

First, I think those students studying the sciences and technical subjects, the subjects that will have practical application in their future jobs, work harder than students studying the humanities. Equally, and probably for the same reason – that such students, later, make a direct contribution to the economy – the standards in the sciences and scientific research, including medicine, are higher. Overall the standards in the national universities are higher than those in private universities, though in many cases their budgets are far smaller. Of the money the government allots to the national universities each year, about 50 per cent goes to the prestigious Tokyo University, 25 per cent to the prestigious Kyoto University while the remaining twenty-four national universities share the other 25 per cent. The national universities are strangled by petty bureaucracy; professors are poorly paid, have little holiday and must, in theory, get permission to leave the bounds of their city. Again, as far as I have observed, the standards of science are higher than the humanities in national universities. My son visited the laboratories of Kyoto University, having just left the laboratories of Oxford. He was extremely impressed by the quality of the young researchers but said that in one field of research at Kyoto University they had ten men investigating an area where in Oxford they would have had one. This saturation approach is a typical and successful Japanese method of dealing with many problems.

Many of the academics and post-graduate students in every branch of Japanese universities are probably potentially brilliant. Some, however, will have got their jobs largely through exceptionally good memories, others through the nepotism which dominates university appointments. If you look through the faculty lists of my own university, Doshisha, you will find a remarkably inbred situation since 99 per cent of faculty members are Doshisha graduates. In the Department of English Literature where I taught, factions led by influential retired professors, who came down from the hills for the big decisions, carved up the appointments between them. If a young man did not have the support of a strong faction, be he the brightest student ever, he would have no chance of an appointment in the department. Worse than that, however bright a student, should the faculty object to him, he may never get a decent academic job anywhere.

I enjoyed my two years at Doshisha University teaching a strange mixture of English Literature and British Social History, called in Japan 'British Cultural Studies'. My colleagues were kind enough in their remote and reticent way, though it never entered anyone's head to show me around the campus. For two weeks on arrival I sat wondering if there was any kind of library, only to discover that a superb library was situated next door to my office. This was typical of the university's runcible administration. I remember receiving a printed invitation to some university buffet lunch. At the last minute I nearly decided not to go. Fortunately, my conscience pricked me. Arriving at the hall where the lunch was taking place, an anxious-looking official came up to me.

'Lowe-sensei, I am so glad that you have come. You are the guest of honour and you will be answering our President's speech.'

'That's fine,' I said, not unduly worried as I presumed I still had the period of lunch in which to think up something suitable to say.

'Our President is speaking now. You will have to reply in four minutes.'

I put my mind into top gear and four minutes later came out with a string of not altogether sincere platitudes which seemed acceptable. I have learnt that the important thing on such occasions is to say nothing.

The English faculty of Doshisha was typical of a great deal of private university life in Japan. The students did not expect to work hard, nor was it expected of them. After the trauma of getting into university, society allows this four-year holiday before the pressures of adult life, work and marriage. English and American literature were considered polite subjects for girls to study, raising their marriage value provided they did not make the *faux pas* of learning to speak English. My classes, some of which had over 200 students, were about 95 per cent girls and 5 per cent boys; a difficult calculation as some boys never actually appeared. In those classes no more than 30 per cent had a reasonable comprehension of English while not more than 5 per cent took a serious interest in the subject. It would have been more stimulating to teach a class of twelve-year-olds in the United States or Europe.

There are, however, different kinds of challenges and I determined to find a way to make the lectures entertaining and interesting. On the positive side, the students were beautifully behaved, extremely kind, and many of them prepared to take an interest if the lectures were packaged in a way that appealed to them. I used a large number of colour slides which my students charmingly called 'free movies'. As a result of the years spent learning the Chinese characters Japanese develop an extremely visual memory. The Japanese 'see' their language while English speakers largely 'hear' theirs. I noticed that whenever in the exams I based a question on one of the slides, almost always every student gave the right answer.

Students will never speak in class and to ask direct questions is unkind. The first morning I faced my graduate seminar I could tell after quarter of an hour that it was a farce. Classroom discussion was impossible and I was confronted with fifteen mature students each with different interests. I announced that I was switching the seminar to a tutorial system and would be happy to give each student one hour a week when they could pursue a subject of their choice. Five students dropped out with dismay, ten students stayed with me, a few for two years, several of them becoming and remaining good friends. The news went round the faculty like wildfire. This eccentric foreigner who could dispose of his graduate class in ninety minutes was voluntarily going to spend ten hours a week with them. Such a show of enthusiasm was not popular. In a university department you are wise to do exactly what you are asked and no more. Enthusiasm, initiative, imagination are all alien and disruptive.

On another occasion initiative led me into trouble in the university. The story illustrates a number of points about the pressures of Japanese life. Doshisha is a commercial organisation which must attract parents to pay its high fees. People like me are employed largely to allow the insertion in their brochures of the words, 'Oxford University'. I sometimes felt they might have been wiser to have used my degree and asked me to stay at home. Their brochure also offers all students a certain amount of instruction in English, guaranteeing one year of English conversation classes conducted by what in Japan is called 'a native speaker'. This sets a problem for the department responsible for organising these classes as the student body is huge and a great many 'native speakers' must be found. One of the organisers, an able assistant professor in the English Language Department – totally separate from my own faulty – asked if I would take some conversation classes. Reluctantly I agreed, on condition that my son, who was staying with me, could share the classes.

It is necessary to go back a year in order to introduce the main character in this story. During the summer before I was due to start teaching at Doshisha, I received a letter from the faculty chairman asking if I could do something for one of his younger colleagues who was spending a sabbatical year at an English university. We invited this Doshisha professor to stay at home. He spoke good English, was intelligent and seemingly pleasant. I recall some incidents during his two visits which provide clues to his later behaviour. One evening he gave us a sudden emotional outburst about how he felt inferior as a Japanese. Later he told me about the students at Doshisha, how badly behaved they were, how I must not be disappointed that few would attend my classes, and how I must not be surprised by the low standards. The last was true, but his other remarks were completely false.

We put quite a lot of planning into the conversation courses and spent some money on tapes, books and a huge range of popular magazines which we had been told would be refunded but never was. The classes were doomed to failure. I challenge anyone to run a successful English conversation class with thirty conscripts who do not speak in class. It was very different to the pleasures of teaching the English literature students. Two or three times I told the assistant professor how my son and I were getting on. Then it happened. I was working in my office one morning when the assistant professor came in, looking embarrassed.

'I'm afraid there is some trouble with your classes.'

'Trouble? How do you mean?'

'Someone has complained about your son teaching. In theory there is a rule that nobody may teach in the university unless they have a master's degree.'

'But you and your department knew that he was taking part in these classes.'

'It would not have mattered if there had not been no complaint. Strangely, it came from your faculty, not ours.'

'Who made the complaint?'

'It was M.–sensei.' He named the young professor who had stayed with us in England. I was amazed. 'I cannot understand it,' my friend said, 'and he is making a tremendous fuss and threatening to take the matter to our faculty committee if your son does not stop teaching.'

I was angry. My son had put a great deal of work into these classes and if we were getting any reaction, it was entirely due to him. The business of the master's degree was rather ironic in this academic nurseryland. Although young, my son was possibly better qualified academically than most people who taught at Doshisha. Finally, I was dismayed by M.-sensei, our former guest. Since he had returned to Doshisha I had learned things about him that could explain his outbursts in England and maybe this present attack on my son. A number of people, both faculty members and my students, had dropped hints that M.-sensei was not Japanese but a Korean. If this were true he may have had a cruel life fighting discrimination all the way into his present job. At that time Koreans were banned from academic posts at national universities though the law has since been changed. But like many persecuted people, M.-sensei was incapable of keeping a low profile. He over-dressed, talked too much, was bossy and was what the Japanese call *kiza*, or pretentious. He was disliked in the department but nobody could give him a fair retort for fear of being considered prejudiced. The misery on my colleague's face showed that there could be unpleasant trouble ahead.

'Sensei, I don't quite understand? Everyone in your faculty knew that my son was teaching. We made no secret of it. There have been no complaints from the students. Why not let M.-sensei go to your faculty committee? I am perfectly prepared to explain the situation.'

'We cannot let him go to the committee. It would make great trouble for you.'

The use of the word 'you' took me in one step to the heart of the matter. If my friend had used the word 'us', it might have been more accurate and honest. Seeing the way the wind was blowing, already reddening the embers of the scapegoats' sacrificial fire, I suggested that he let me think the matter over for twenty-four hours. I hoped that it all might have blown over by the next day.

Later, walking down the corridor I was waylaid by a small, sad-eyed professor whom I had often seen but had never met. He was the Chairman of the English Language Department. He drew me to one side.

'Ah, Lowe-sensei, this is a most serious matter.'

'I don't find it very serious. My son and I are doing exactly what we agreed to do and your department was fully informed. I should be very happy to explain the situation to your department's committee if anyone wishes to complain to them.'

The professor paled.

'It must not go to the committee. It is a very serious matter.'

'Could you explain to me why it is so serious?'

The professor gave me a searching look.

'It is a matter of money', he said, in the tone of voice of one who has said the last word on the subject.

'What . . .?'

'Yes, this is a professional matter. You are being paid for these classes. Money is involved. That is why it is serious.'

He looked so pathetically smarmy. Now we had moved off the slippery slopes of ethics onto the solid ground of money. Or so he thought. But foolishly he had not done his homework.

'Sensei, it's strange you should wish to make this a matter of money. You say we are being paid for these classes. My son and I have been teaching for over two months and so far we have not received one yen. Before you take that line, you might like to consult with your administration.'

I have seldom seen a man so instantly deflated. The 'ace of spades' turned into a 'two of diamonds' before his eyes, and I left him dazed and mumbling.

After a bad night's sleep my mood was not conciliatory the next morning when my friend came to see me.

'We must do something quickly. M.-sensei is determined to go to our committee. I cannot understand why he is interfering. It is no concern of his.'

'Well, everyone in his department knows that he is a difficult person.'

My friend was too cautious to comment on such an outspoken opinion.

'Frankly,' I said, 'I'm fed up with the whole business. I've decided that it would be best if someone else took over our classes immediately.'

'That is out of the question.' My friend looked more worried than ever. 'Such a change would have to be taken to the committee. You must continue until the end of the year.'

'No, I've made up my mind. I only took on the classes at your request. I have too much work already and they have been a tiresome burden. I shall be delighted to hand over to someone else.'

'That is out of the question for you', he said in a cold voice.

19 A family welcome at the rural *minshuku*

20 Instant traditional food in a chain Chinese restaurant, Kyoto

21 A Meiji hospital at
Saiseikan, Yamagata,
1878

WESTERN INFLUENCE—
OLD AND NEW

22 Tokyo's newest skyscraper
hotel, the Akasaka Prince,
1983

'For me?'

'Yes, you cannot afford to do it.' He leaned over me to make his point. 'It will damage your future career here.'

I pointed out, that as I was leaving forever in about three months, that was an extremely ineffective form of argument, and that I did not care for being pressured anyway. He saw his mistake and adopted a less aggressive tone.

'You must realise that the department has no objection to your son teaching and had it not been for this outside interference we were completely happy. However, we are forced to say something to M.-sensei to keep him quiet. It would be enough if we could assure him that you will attend every class, even if you only go in for the first few minutes.'

I went home and tried to sort my thoughts into a more Japanese perspective. I realised that both my friend and the chairman of his department were frightened, not about my future career, but about some black mark on their record. It was understandable and not their fault. Relenting, I telephoned and said I would do whatever they wished to resolve the situation.

To this day I do not know what motivated M.-sensei. I saw and spoke to him often after this episode and he never let drop a hint that he knew anything about it. Possibly he saw in my son all the opportunities his nationality had denied him and the business at Doshisha may have been some obscure form of jealousy. The episode shows how easily the boat is rocked in any Japanese organisation if one person ignores the ground-rules.

The story, with all its absurdity, hypocrisy, bureaucracy and lack of open debate is characteristic of Japanese university life. I read in the press, as I write, that the Prime Minister wishes for an educational system which will 'nurture people who conform to a universal moral norm and have high ideals, physical strength, individuality and creativity'. Should the Japanese educational system ever get around to producing such people, they will need to restructure society to contain them.

These last few pages have had a negative tone. It is the system which is negative. Japanese people are innately intelligent, exceptionally lively, and extremely creative. But, be they professors or be they Junior High School students, the present system as shaped by Japanese society stultifies many of their natural abilities to produce a people who are as bland as their food. Japan is very small and has many people. In their own way the Japanese have learned how to live with that situation. Put twenty-five people in a small open-boat in a rough sea and they soon learn to sit still. The trouble is that creative people and individualists tend to be restless.

7

Happiness is Gold

OSAKA, KOBE, WAKAYAMA AND HYOGO

To my shame I have never come to grips with Osaka, Japan's third-largest city with a population of about 2.5 million, a port handling some 40 per cent of Japan's export trade, and the administrative, industrial and commercial centre of western Honshu. It is largely a concrete city with a reconstructed concrete castle. I like its outgoing people and its lavish food but Umeda must be the most confusing railway terminus in the world and outside, mile upon mile, the confusion grows worse, a maze of anonymous areas criss-crossed by rivers and canals. Indeed, where does Osaka begin and end? As I leave Kyoto on the Hankyu line, the train speeds through unending if rather fascinating suburbs until suddenly we are in Osaka. A few stations bear names with historical associations but mostly history has been buried under the new suburban buildings which press so close that there is hardly room for the train to pass.

In Osaka you have the choice of a gloomy subway, characterless streets or raised expressways which offer a bird's-eye view of the dirty concrete and the dirtier water of the rivers and canals. I used to enjoy the bustle of the entertainment area around Dotombori and the excellent arcaded shopping across the canal, but really I prefer Kyoto's version of such tourist fun. There are some good museums and the early historical memories enshrined in the Shitennoji Temple but Osaka is full of ghosts.

The city became important when Hideyoshi made it a leading commercial centre at the end of the sixteenth century. It had good water transport facilities and shipped goods up the river to Kyoto. It flourished as a merchant centre right up to the Second World War, when, in 1940, its population was 3.25 million people. The great merchant houses ruled like princes with their own customs, their own geisha quarter and their own dialect, even their private fire brigades. Although there are still many rich merchants in Osaka today, they add little to the colour or the culture of contemporary Japan.

The bunraku national puppet theatre, if they are playing, makes a visit to Osaka worthwhile; essential if you are seriously interested in theatre. In 1984 a new theatre was opened which got off to an unhappy start. During the performance, a technician, confused by the new controls, pressed the wrong button, set half the fire sprinkler system going, and created a major rainstorm among the front rows of the stalls. Fortunately, the newspapers assured readers, none of the puppets was damaged. The very word 'puppet' conjures up in many people's minds some form of entertainment for children. Rest assured that bunraku is as adult as it is enthralling.

Puppet plays began to flourish at the beginning of the seventeenth century, exactly when the popular merchant class theatre of kabuki had its first beginnings. The puppet theatre grew out of a long tradition of story-telling accompanied by the Japanese lute and later the three-stringed samisen. As in Elizabethan London, the authorities saw the professional theatre as a hotbed of lawlessness and vice, particularly the encouragement of sodomy with the boy actors who appeared after women had been banned from the stage. Throughout the seventeenth century the kabuki suffered more and more restrictions until the peculiar situation was reached at the beginning of the eighteenth century when Japan's greatest playwrights such as Chikamatsu (1653–1724) and Sosuke Namiki (1695–1751) wrote not for actors but for the puppets of bunraku. It had built a great popular following, was free of the limitations and difficulties surrounding kabuki, and the puppeteers had achieved such a dramatic range through their puppets that in certain ways they could achieve effects unobtainable by human actors. It is interesting that when the puppet theatre declined later in the eighteenth century the masterpieces of the kabuki theatre were and still are the great puppet plays.

Chikamatsu is often called the Shakespeare of Japan.

The bunraku (named after Bunrakuken Uemura, an eighteenth-century promoter of the tradition) puppets are about two-thirds life size, have articulated limbs and complicated mechanisms for facial expressions and are operated by three men who stand dressed in black with the puppet on the stage. Generally the chief operator is in charge of the body, face and right hand. One assistant works the left hand and the other both the legs. Women puppets have no legs but the assistant looks after the skirt of her kimono. Described in that way, it makes a performance sound absurd, particularly as in many scenes there may be four puppets and twelve black-hooded operators on the stage, not to mention a black-hooded props man quietly preparing some quick-change or special effect which both bunraku and kabuki like to employ. Just as Shakespeare made few concessions in creating Lady Macbeth or Juliet or Cleopatra to the fact that these parts were to be played by boys, so the bunraku dramatists wrote fully rounded plays, rich in action and characterisation and reaching emotional climaxes of thwarted love and suicide. Had it been otherwise, the plays would not have converted so perfectly to the kabuki theatre and human actors. I can only say that it works. I first saw bunraku in London when I took two theatrical friends who knew nothing about Japan. For the first fifteen minutes I was uncomfortably aware of the operators, though they were impressively impassive. By half-way through the performance I only half-noticed the hooded puppeteers and, in an indefinable way, their presence, their silent dedication, and their identification with the character they were creating, all added an intensity to the drama. They became an integral part of the performance. The play ended with a deeply moving love scene and a mutual suicide between the two young lovers. As I write my memory clearly sees two people on that stage; not two puppets and six puppeteers. That is the magic of bunraku.

For over one hundred years Kobe has been one of the leading foreign settlements in Japan. Kobe is today Japan's greatest port. It was opened in 1868 to foreign trade and soon became a prosperous settlement of foreigners. Kobe enjoys a beautiful position along the coast with forested mountains rising steeply behind the city. It is also blessed with a mild climate. A model of the nineteenth-century town in the Kobe City Museum shows what a charming, even elegant, place it must have been, and the objects in this museum recall the life and experiences of foreigners in Japan from the time of the sixteenth-century Jesuit missionaries to the more complacent lives of the Victorian merchants. Now this old town has disappeared under a frenzy of narrow shopping streets and arcades and a new development down by the port called 'Portopia', promoted as a 'city for the future'. Kobe struggles in rivalry with Osaka and likes to play the role of Japan's international city. I see little more than a Japanese town with a scattering of Indian restaurants, a few exceptionally good bread shops and, if you want to step back for a moment into a kind of expatriate past, somewhat frayed around the edges, there is always the Kobe Club. To the east of the Kobe Club run two or three streets containing foreign mansions from the Meiji and Taisho periods, several of which have been rather over-restored and turned into museums, boutiques and a Chinese restaurant. It has become a popular sightseeing round for Japanese tourists and, if nothing else, the houses do give some idea of the style of those times. It is sad that they have not been better protected by the city and that their restoration has been left to commercial users. The area also contains a synagogue, a mosque and other monuments pointing to the mixed backgrounds of its inhabitants. It is a pleasant, lively town and the people are noticeably tolerant of foreigners.

To the north and west of Kobe lies the prefecture of Hyogo and to the south of Osaka the prefecture of Wakayama. In each area is one of my most favourite places in Japan so I shall divide the limited space I have between those two, starting with Japan's finest and most handsome castle in the attractive town of Himeji. The Japanese have given Himeji Castle, with its towering white walls rising gently over the surrounding trees, a suitably romantic name: 'White Heron Castle'. Today the castle stands, like a bird poised for flight, in a large park and on the outer walls and around the moats wild flowers have been allowed to grow so that as you pass through the outer courts and up the steps to the great five-storeyed main donjon, you pass through an enchanted garden, strangely at odds with the martial purpose of the architecture but nonetheless beautiful. Himeji Castle is recognised as the finest and most complete in Japan. There was originally a castle built here in 1346 but the present castle dates from 1601 though it was added to on the western side later. A sensitive restoration was carried out between 1957 and 1964. The castle has its main donjon, three smaller keeps, all joined by covered passageways, and a huge complex of inner and outer courtyards and connecting stairways. The white walls and the simple square and bell-shaped windows set off the strong but graceful design of the grey-tiled roofs, their line varying between carefully balanced peaked-gables and undulating ones (Plate 12). Inside the enormous polished planks of the donjon floors and the massive carpentry, with perilously steep staircases leading up, are magnificently impressive, like the handiwork of giants. From the upper levels the roof design can be seen in complex patterns. It is one of those buildings that seems perfect from every viewpoint. I am not normally an enthusiast for fortified architecture but I went to Himeji Castle for an hour, as recommended by the guide-book, and I stayed the whole day. There was so much to see and enjoy.

If you have a few days to spare in late autumn after the Japanese tourists have all gone home, I don't think you will be disappointed in the sacred Buddhist mountain retreat of Koya-san, hidden in the mountains due east of Wakayama. More than a million pilgrims come here every year but when I went late in October, the place was pleasantly deserted. The summer is the most popular season as pilgrims can then combine their devotions with a day or two of cool mountain air. It is entirely a religious centre and mercifully has escaped too much commercialisation. It is wise to book your accommodation in advance and, unless you have a car, the mountain can be ascended only by a cable-car which carries one up to the little station from where buses run to various destinations. It is one of those places more easily visited with a Japanese-speaking friend but that is not essential.

Along the east side of the Takamine mountains at about 900 m runs a plateau 5.5 km from east to west and 2.2 km from north to south. This great platform is cradled and concealed in the Koya-Ryujin forest. Here the great Buddhist priest, Kobo-Daishi (774–835), teacher of esoteric Shingon Buddhism, built a monastery in 816. The followers of the Shingon sect are more fervent than most Japanese Buddhists. All Shingon temples have a special atmosphere with their elaborate rites centring on the fire ritual and other esoteric practices. The faithful believe that in 835 their beloved founder entered the *Okunoin*, the sacred heart of Koya-san, and fell into meditation and that within that rustic building in the grove of Cryptomeria Kobo-Daishi still lives in a state of deep meditation. Pilgrims crouch at the fence that separates them from the *Okunoin*, clutching their rosaries and muttering their devotions. It is a place hallowed by prayer.

Within this mountain retreat is a small town, two main groups of temples and all around about a hundred monasteries large and small of which about fifty offer simple but pleasant accommodation to pilgrims and visitors. Many of these monasteries have handsome buildings and charming gardens and it provides a good opportunity to stay in a wholly traditional Japanese atmosphere. Most of the monastic hostels have a morning service which it is polite to attend and foolish not to as it gives a glimpse of Shingon worship. It is a peaceful place to wander around and requires at least two days to do it justice, more if you really wish to absorb the atmosphere and use it to relax the mind and body.

One experience in Koya-san stands out in my mind. The walk from the entrance of the great burial ground to the court before the *Okunoin* is about 2 km. Go early before the crowds and while the early sun slants in huge rays through the cedars. Take the upper and quieter path, looking over the huge jumble of stone tombs below (Plate 16) and to the left a seeming ruined city of tombs running up the mountainside, shadowed by trees and undergrowth or brightened by the sweep of the sunlight. There are thousands of tombstones here, tombs of emperors and feudal lords and more humble graves, dating back to the Kamakura period. Pillars, stupas, obelisks, and row upon row of standing and seated figures of Jizo, the guardian of children, comic in cotton hats and bibs, with charming weatherworn faces (Plate 17). Each time I photographed one, I immediately found another I liked more. It was a place of great beauty, the sun and the growing warmth of the clear autumn morning making the burial ground solemn but not gloomy.

Each Sunday morning a small advertisement twinkles at me from the front page of my newspaper – 'Happiness is Gold'. Those three words have a lot to say about Japanese post-war materialism and the outlook it has created both in everyday life and in the world of big business. Osaka, as a great mercantile and industrial centre, seems a suitable starting point for the consideration of this subject. In that great merchant city the normal daily greeting used to be '*Mokarimakka?*' ('Is your business going well?')

Japan was ruined at the end of the Second World War and its people were near starvation. Forty years later Japan is the greatest economic power after the United States, despite its almost total lack of raw materials and natural resources. Today it even imports 40 per cent of its food. That is the Japanese economic miracle which peaked in the 1960s and 1970s but has also stood up well to the 'oil shock' and the international recession of the last few years. Japan has also enjoyed certain advantages. It was forced totally to rebuild its industry, and it has had far less defence costs than most other industrial nations. But in the end the only real explanations for Japan's economic success are good management and hard work, a formula that has proved equally successful in other highly disciplined oriental societies such as South Korea, Taiwan, Hong Kong and Singapore.

The disciplines demanded to create the Japanese economic miracle are severe and would be intolerable to most modern western societies, though they might not have seemed so strange to the pre-war working class. I believe that Japanese management can make these demands of people because the Japanese put security beyond any other consideration; financial security and the social security that springs from it. In large and small ways Japanese struggle to keep their lives safe. Most Japanese will sacrifice anything for the sake of security.

It is only fair to remember that the whole nature of Japanese society leaves little room for individual manoeuvre or survival outside the group. It is hard to 'drop out' in Japan because there is nowhere to go. A few brave and bohemian spirits do make their own way, but usually the various dreams are sooner or later exchanged for a safe marriage and the hope that the company bonuses will be good this year. Japanese society is not sympathetic to the non-conformer, certainly once he or she is through university, and there are few public assistance schemes and other western safety-nets. There are only the park benches around Shinjuku or a cardboard carton under the bridges of Kyoto; neither a romantic prospect.

This book is not a manual on how to do business in Japan, but doing business here over a long period I have learned some lessons which might be of interest to others while throwing some light on the ways business works in Japan. Particular cases, although limited, are often more revealing than general theorising, and more convincing. I would start by saying that doing business in Japan is exceptionally difficult and requires unusual patience, both in the short and the long term. The Japanese themselves do not on the whole look for quick profits and the foreign businessman would be wise to adopt the same attitude. Allied to that, the Japanese are less naïve than they were fifteen years ago. They now know exactly what they want in every field and how to get it. The art market, to take but one example, got away with murder when the Japanese first began buying western art and antiques. I remember arriving at the Tokyo offices of a company I used to work for and at midday I was led proudly to the new senior manager's dining room, furnished since my last visit with antiques from London. The tour of inspection of the furniture and paintings included the prices and I was mortified. The room could equally well have been described as the 'Chamber of Rubbish' or the 'Chamber of Horrors', with Jack-the-Ripoff as the perpetrator. I do not think any western businessman would get away with that today.

However, the question of honest dealing is by no means one-sided. Japan has an extraordinary double-standard of honesty. In ordinary, everyday life it remains one of the most honest countries in the world. I never count my change here and as far as I know at shop and personal level, in eighteen years I have never been cheated once. I should add that daily money matters are so arranged in Japan that it would not be easy to cheat. Everything is on a cash basis and virtually everything is paid for on the nail. But I still think that among ordinary Japanese people there remains an unusually high standard of honesty which makes it a restful place to live.

I cannot say the same of the business world. Here I would tend to apply that cynical adage, 'Believe nothing you are told, and get it in writing'. There are, to be sure, many wholly honest Japanese businessmen, but maybe there is an underlying attitude that 'all is fair in love and business'. The Japanese are extremely pragmatic and I think the west should perhaps wake up to the realities of the Japanese market place about which they often remain almost sentimental. Modern business, for better or worse, has much of the character of war, complete with industrial espionage. It is better to face the fact that the Japanese are out to win, and in order to win they will do anything they think they can get away with. I once told a Tokyo friend about a trick a western publisher had played on me. 'How clever,' she said. 'Just like a Japanese publisher.'

The long saga of 'trade friction' over the imbalance of pay-ments between the United States and the EEC and Japan often assumes all the unreality of grand opera. Nero fiddled while Rome burned. Future history books may tell of how the President of the United States fussed about beef and oranges while Detroit went up in smoke. On the Japanese side the response is hardly less cosmetic. The truth is that Japan has operated extensive tariff barriers, but far more important, it has buried a great deal of foreign competition in the intricacies of normal Japanese bureaucratic import regulations and the maze of the retail and distribution trade in this country which has bankrupted many small Japanese companies besides totally confusing the foreign importer.

There are other realities. Japan needs expertise in all fields, but they learn quickly and why should they continue to employ the foreign expert once they have milked him dry. That is a good business sense, if painful for the expert. Some years ago I was working as a consultant for a fashion company in Tokyo. They were about to celebrate some anniversary and they asked me to organise a suitable 'event' for the occasion. After long negotiations I agreed to mount two fashion design seminars for them, bringing an expert out from England. Knowing what was likely to happen, I charged a stiff fee for our services. Not long before we were due to leave for Japan I received a letter from the company asking if it would be possible to put on a third seminar. It was obvious that the other two were sold out, but despite that the second half of the letter asked, in absurdly sentimental terms, if we could lighten the severe burden on the students by giving this seminar at a reduced fee. I replied that we should be delighted to give the third seminar at identical rates to the first two, and that was immediately accepted.

Although the seminars were my idea and I had spent one and a half years organising them, once they were set up I did not have an important part to play. They had hardly started before the president of the company was trying to negotiate with my colleague from London for future seminars, expertise, books and I know not what. My colleague was kind enough to keep me informed and to refer the president back to me, but I did not really mind. It was exactly what I had expected and the reason why I was asking a high fee while I was still necessary to the company. Foreign experts have a limited life here and they are wise to charge accordingly. Nor indeed do the Japanese object to paying high fees if they are getting the advice they require.

If asked what I thought the golden rule might be for those wishing to sell their goods in Japan, I think I would reply, 'Never try to sell the Japanese anything they don't want.' That may sound very obvious, but in the west we spend a considerable amount of time, money and energy successfully selling to people things they don't really want. Japanese industry and commerce may apply the same methods to their own markets, but the Japanese buyer knows what he can sell, by whatever methods, and he will not fall victim to the 'soft sell' himself. Once, quite inadvertently, I got myself into this situation with a number of peculiar results.

I had mounted two successful exhibitions for Seibu Department Stores and when I next came to Tokyo I went to a meeting to discuss the possibility of a third exhibition at their Ikebukuro store. From the moment I entered the room I knew that they had some special request. Special was certainly the word. Seibu wanted The Beatles, regardless of the fact that The Beatles had split up. It took me two days to persuade my Seibu colleagues that neither they nor anyone else were going to bring The Beatles together again for a series of concerts in Tokyo, or anywhere else. Amazingly, my colleagues really gave me the feeling that I was holding out on them. Recently, by a stroke of luck, I had managed to get some of the decorations from Pall Mall for the Emperor's State visit to London, at forty-eight hours notice. This had so impressed them that they took it for granted that mustering a famous ex-pop group was a mere nothing. For once the Japanese sense of hierarchy was a little off balance.

Eventually my colleagues said that their basic ambition was to put on an exhibition showing the Japanese public something about young people in Britain. I liked the idea but could see difficulties of putting it into interesting visual terms. I suddenly had the idea of an exhibition of the work of the students of the Royal College of Art, certainly representative of young talent in Britain. By the time I left Tokyo, Seibu were enthusiastic, though I emphasised that for maximum impact the exhibition must be selected from the students' diploma shows the following summer. Seibu agreed.

I approached the Royal College of Art and everyone concerned was excited with the idea, on condition that preparations could start soon. There was only one year before the exhibition was to take place. I was shortly back in Tokyo armed with a lot of information and photographs showing the work of past students. Seibu, with seeming enthusiasm, agreed to go ahead. Once we had agreed on the exhibition, Seibu began asking when they could come to London to see and choose the exhibits. I explained for the third time that there would be nothing to see until the diploma shows the following summer. The committee looked glum. I then explained that the Royal College must employ a secretary immediately to get the preparations under way and to give help to the organiser and designer. This would mean that the Royal College would need £1000 immediately. Everyone looked uncomfortably out of the window. It seemed that it would be hard to find the money immediately as the whole scheme had not yet been approved by the accounts department. As Seibu are the largest private company in Japan it seemed strange that they could not muster £1000 but I was determined not to let the exhibition founder now that it was off the ground. But I also knew that the Royal College must have the money, so I offered to Seibu that I lend the Royal College the money, provided that Seibu paid me back in two months. Agreement seemed to have been reached and I returned to London.

The Royal College went to work and shortly they were bombarding me with questions which needed answers from Tokyo. I wrote a number of letters to Seibu, none of which was answered, and by the time the two months were up, I had not been repaid my interest-free loan. So I sat down and wrote a letter to the owner and president of Seibu whom I had met on a number of occasions. Of course, I doubted if the letter would ever get to him, but I hoped that the process of interception might cause the necessary explosion . . . it did.

At 5.30 in the morning, five days after I had posted the letter, there was a frantic telephone call from my department. First I got the sentimental touch. How could I write such a letter? Easily, I replied. Then the threatening touch. If the chairman knew you had written to the president, he would never speak to you again. So what . . . he's already not writing, so not speaking won't add much. Then the results. If all my letters were answered immediately, and all letters answered in the future, and if the money were cabled that morning, would I allow my letter to be destroyed without their president seeing it. Agreed.

Now the letters began to flow from Seibu and nearly every one reflected a growing neurosis about their inability to see the objects which were going to make up the exhibition. Assurances, letters, sketch plans, photographs, nothing had a calming effect and when I next returned to Tokyo I could tell at once that there was a deep malaise among the exhibition team. We were touching the very root nerves of Japanese security. Infinitely better an exhibition of fifth-rate Renoirs than the hope of something brilliant but unknown. The paintings may be terrible but in Japan it is the name that counts. Though to be absolutely fair to Seibu they normally not only had the top names but also top quality exhibitions of the artists' work. In this case they were frightened by the unknown, something that the Japanese have no experience of working with.

We had a few gloomy meetings and after one I was drawn aside. I was told that they were deeply worried about the success of this exhibition and they now wondered if, in return for a handsome cash payment to the Royal College, I could persuade them to cancel the exhibition. While I could sympathise with Seibu's nervousness, the whole exhibition had been sparked off by them, the difficulties had been clearly explained at the start and the Royal College had by now put a great deal of work into it. Beyond that the students were excited by the idea of doing a big show in Tokyo and the exhibition had already received wide publicity in London. I told the committee that the exhibition must go on. I did remind them that I had already produced two successful exhibitions for them and I had no intention of letting them down now if they would give me sufficient faith and backing to carry it through.

To Seibu's enormous credit they never looked back from that moment and gave me the warmest support. And with the opening of the summer diploma shows their enthusiasm awoke and they mounted a most handsome exhibition and treated the visiting team with their usual generosity. But it was a miserable few months for me and I determined that never again would I try to sell anything in Japan unless I had a totally willing buyer.

Those who are impressed with the reliability of the goods exported from Japan – and surely mass-production quality control is Japan's most original contribution to the industrial world, as well as the network of back-up services they have created around the world – should realise that on the home market the consumer does not always receive such kid-glove treatment. On the whole here consumer goods are excellent, though I did work my way through two Japanese typewriters in three months. Gaining no satisfaction locally, I telephoned the head office in Tokyo. They asked me if I typed much, to which I replied a great deal. Ah well, they explained, the expensive type-writer I had bought was meant only for typing a few letters and things like that. Unfortunately, this significant fact was not published in the brochure or anywhere else.

Behind a veneer of extreme politeness, with uniformed girls bowing at the foot of every department store escalator, in many respects the Japanese public are ripped off (only that phrase is brutal enough) partly because many of them are the victims of their own snobbery and ignorance; partly because the wholesale and retail trade is a jungle; and partly because, in this authorit-arian society, anyone in the slightest position of authority is an expert and in Japan you blindly follow the expert. Certain services, such as the banks, would be without a customer in a week in the west. The main service they seem to offer is to themselves. Worst of all, because of the nature of Japanese society, it has proved impossible to form effective consumer protection associations. If you are trying to complain with one side of your mouth, and to apologise with the other, it leaves little room for teeth.

Another common myth is that Japan is the land of devoted

23 Good service in a traditional Kyoto shop

STYLES OF SERVICE—OLD AND NEW

24 Self-service in a modern department store

25 Hiroshima, a remnant of the holocaust

POINT OF NO RETURN

26 A new Japan: posters for the local cinema supported on the wall of a Buddhist cemetery

craftsmanship, each plumber and electrician applying spanner and screwdriver with a Zen-like concentration. The truth is that most of these craftsmen have one main genius; getting the job badly done in the fastest time before the bleeper bleeps in their breast pocket summoning them to their next job. They mostly work under intense pressure. My main drain went recently and the plumber arrived to repair it, after dark by torchlight. The next week the other end of the drainage system went and this time the plumber did a short-circuit job by daylight. As he was leaving he noticed a rusty stand pipe by the east wall of the house. Kindly but unwisely, and against my advice as it looked 'live' to me, he removed it with two well-aimed blows of a sledgehammer. I sleep down that end of the house and the following morning when I woke I was depressed to hear torrential rain thrashing against the house. I got up and slid back one of the wooden shutters. Overnight I had acquired a 3-m-high fountain, beautiful but ill-placed. I could tell several stories of that kind but I will summarise my feelings by saying that now I never leave the house for a moment when Japanese workmen are here. I like to keep a constant eye on them.

Whether you consider the step from commerce to crime a long or a short one will depend on your own point of view. Certainly in Japan, organised crime or the *yakuza* gangs do run certain commercial activities and in recent years bribery and corruption have become more widespread in the business world. It must be said straightaway that Japan has the lowest crime rate of any industrial country in the world and the general trend is for that rate to go down. What crime there is tends to be peculiarly Japanese. The majority of murders are committed within families: a father deep in debt kills his wife and child and kills himself; the occasional student runs amok and kills a parent under the extreme pressure of Japanese life; and from time to time gang warfare breaks out and gangsters shoot each other. The police are most efficient in Japan and the number of arrests, confessions and convictions are high. In this close-knit society it is difficult to hide, while the high rate of confessions may be explained partly by the fact that under Japanese law the police may hold and question a suspect for several days before the suspect is allowed to contact anyone.

In the last few years Japan has been dismayed by its increasing juvenile delinquency. In 1983 the police were summoned to keep order at the commencement ceremonies of one out of every six Junior High Schools in Japan. Violence against teachers rose 26 per cent in 1983, with many girl offenders, 93 per cent of all cases being in Junior High Schools. Most amazingly, in such a family-oriented society, of the 579 runaways picked up by the police in 1983, only 6.5 per cent of cases had been reported by the parents. At the same time drug-taking and glue-sniffing increased and, most untypically, some boys and girls beat three vagrants to death in Yokohama.

Although all this pales almost into insignificance compared with the situation in the United States and Europe, it has worried Japanese society, and particularly those involved with education. It is significant that so many of the offenders come from Junior High School (12–15) when the pressures of work are strong but they are not yet wholly absorbed by the university entrance exams. A friend of mine, who teaches Japanese literature at a particularly tough state school in Tokyo and spends most of the time educating his boys by teaching them soccer, said to me that it is useless to blame the children. Society has created their problems and society must solve them.

Japanese society is so all-embracing that it dislikes anything to exist in isolation. In Japan, if the workers form a trade union, slowly and inevitably it is absorbed until it is little more than a department of that company, its officials on the company payroll. Even the large, leftish unions such as the teachers', for all the noise they make, seem to lack real muscle, and the annual furore which takes place each year when town after town refuses to accommodate their conference has become little more than another of the summer rituals.

The same is true of organised crime, which is carefully fitted into society, its members identified and recorded, the perimeters of its operations more or less defined by the police. Arms and drug smuggling are absolute taboo and successfully controlled. But there was a bizarre incident last year when it was discovered that certain *yakuza*, so desperately short of guns, had somehow organised the metalworking shop of a prison in Kyushu into producing primitive handguns. The *yakuza*, who keep very much to themselves, are behind much of the small-time gambling that is winked at by the police, prostitution, protection rackets, strong-arm action for the loan sharks and, where they can get away with it, drugs. The police usually know exactly what they are up to and do not interfere unless the gangs trespass outside their allotted areas or when jealousy and greed leads to rival gang-warfare. With their luridly tattooed bodies and their secret societies they are frequently romanticised but for the most part their way of life is wholly unadmirable, and unromantic.

8

Hiroshima and After

WESTERN HONSHU: CHUGOKU

It was pouring with rain as we drove up the west shore of Lake Biwa. This was a backdoor into Chugoku, but at the north end of the lake it brought us to a famous stretch of the Japan Sea. Typically, we had just enjoyed a week of golden late September weather. The dark rain reinforced the frustrations of driving in Japan. The lake looked sullen as the sky, and in the mountains beyond, the narrow, wet roads wound monotonously through the low clouds. But whatever the frustrations, a car enables one to reach remoter places poorly served by public transport and frees one from restrictive timetables. One can also seek out the more rural *minshuku*, which in the journey ahead were to provide some amusing experiences.

We reached the Japan Sea close to one of the three classical beauty spots of Japan: Amanohashidate, 'The Floating Bridge of Heaven'. The name is taken from Japanese mythology which tells how two gods stood here while they created the islands of Japan. The 'bridge' is, in fact, a sandbar, 3.6 km long and about 100 m wide, which winds across the Bay of Miyazu from the small town of Monju to Fuchu where there is a famous pilgrimage Buddhist temple on the mountainside. When we parked the car in Monju and stood on the shore of the bay, we could see nothing but a line of aged pine trees leading out from the precincts of an old temple across the water into the rainy distance. Standing there in the chilly drizzle, it seemed anything but a beauty spot. Had it not been for the tourist buses parked around our car, I might have thought that we had come to the wrong place.

Wherever you are, Blackpool or Amanohashidate, there is something uniquely dispiriting about resorts in the rain. One is haunted by a sense of what one is missing, and beyond that the tawdry souvenirs and the plastic-tabled cafés take on a special air of desolation. We warmed ourselves with huge bowls of noodles and then wandered into Chionji Temple. The weatherbeaten wooden buildings had a simple charm and a little way off a more elaborate pagoda stood encircled by tall trees. We followed a wide path and suddenly realised that we were walking across 'The Floating Bridge of Heaven' itself. Even here the view was nothing special, but the pines sheltered us from the spitting rain and the old trees were gnarled and knotted by centuries of wind into interesting shapes. I had not realised that it was possible to walk across Amanohashidate. I recommend the walk for the old pines and the sandy beaches with the mountains enclosing the inner Asoumi Lagoon.

But close your eyes to the more recent embellishments of this famous place. The shore of Miyazu Bay is dominated by a glistening-white industrial building, so eye-consuming that it more or less distracts from the other disfigurements scattered along the shore. The lagoon and the mountainside have not been neglected. Here an untidy industrial works scars the view. It is sad but certain proof of Japan's overriding commercialism and insensitivity. Imagine the reaction to a huge gravel works in the centre of Snowdonia, or a five-storey plastics factory on the rim of the Grand Canyon. These architectural warts say much about both official and unofficial attitudes in Japan. It is true that a growing number of Japanese object to such atrocities, but they are as yet incapable of organising effective protest. Recently I saw a sad neighbourhood notice protesting about the construction of a 'love hotel' in that locality, but the notice would achieve nothing.

We took the steamer back from Fuchu to Monju, but even from the boat 'the bridge' remained only a dark line of trees stretching across the bay. But the day had a happy ending. As the boat docked at Monju, the sun came out. We walked through the town, crossed the railway line and came to a small cable-car which takes you up to a viewing station. We had arrived at a perfect moment. The late afternoon sun was fading into twilight. Below lay a magical view. The quiet bay and the lagoon were separated by an undulating bridge of pines, floating across the water. Below us was the circular harbour of Monju and lights began to sparkle all around the water's edge. It is a most beautiful view seen from above, but perhaps one appreciates it more after first walking across 'the bridge' itself. It is always satisfying when disappointment turns to discovery. And our supper of delicious local fish sealed the pleasure of the day.

The Japan Sea coast is generally a wilder and bleaker place than the opposite Pacific shore. In many ways these two seas, with their different natures and climates, have given Japan two faces, each one marked by the features of the neighbouring sea. The wilder coast starts further west and as we started to drive towards Matsue, the coastline remained picturesque with high cliffs and sheltered bays with small wooded islands. I could not say that the area is either remote or wholly unspoilt, but it is attractive with some picturesque fishing villages tucked in among the rocky bays (Plate 4). Follow the coast road around the Okutango Peninsula and you will find a number of fishing ports where the ground floor of all the houses facing the harbour are open to the sea, the families' boats anchored safely beneath their houses. Along the quay the larger boats are moored amidst the usual clutter of nets, black plastic octopus-pots and racks of gutted, drying squid.

The area, slightly inland, is full of caves and hot spring resorts. Coming off the peninsula and driving towards Tottori the coast changes into long sandy beaches, open to the bleak winds that hurl in from the opposite mainland, where angry surf rolls in to the shore. In a few miles the picturesque has given way to poor villages whose small, dilapidated buildings are bleached lifeless by the weather. They must be desolate places when the winter storms come, an empty world of sand and wind, though in places the long stretches of coast whitened by the surf are magnificent.

We were aiming for Matsue, an attractively situated town with the large Lake Shinji to the west and Nakaumi Lagoon to the east. Matsue is the Japanese town most closely associated with the great writer and Japanophile, Lafcadio Hearn (1850–1904).

However, his association with Matsue has been grossly inflated. It is true that he came here when he first arrived in Japan in 1890 to teach English in a local school, but in November, after only seven months' residence, he decided that the Matsue winter would be too cold for him and he moved to Kyushu. Nevertheless, Matsue has made the most of that short residence. Near the castle is the charming samurai house where he lived and, alongside, a museum and a memorial hall. The house captures an echo of his stay in this remote place and has charming gardens which he commemorated in an essay. It is an intriguing glimpse of the Meiji past.

At the far end of Lake Shinji is Izumo Taisha, the oldest Shinto shrine in Japan (Plate 13). In a different way, it is as impressive and interesting as the ancient shrines of Ise and was for me one of the highlights of this visit to Chugoku. Shinto gods tend to have long names, difficult to remember, and for that reason I have so far omitted them. The Izumo Taisha shrine is dedicated to Okuninushi-no-Mikoto, the god said to have introduced farming, sericulture and medicine to Japan. According to mythology the Taisha shrine was originally the palace of this deity. Its style of architecture is almost certainly based on the earliest form of Japanese domestic architecture. The shrines at Ise, always linked with the Imperial family, show the earliest forms of religious architecture and there are marked differences between the two ancient shrines. Centuries ago the Taisha shrine was much larger but the older buildings were destroyed long ago. The present main shrine was built in 1744 while most of the other buildings date from 1874. But the buildings make an impressive group set against the darkly wooded slopes of the Yakumo Hill.

The main approach to the shrine is along an avenue lined with pine trees. At the end of the avenue there is a large open space in front of the steps and gateway leading into the inner shrine. The square building of the main shrine dominates the fenced sacred enclosure, the heavy roof and X-shaped terminals of the roof ridge towering above the surrounding buildings and standing out massively against the background of the surrounding hills. As in so many shrines, both large and small, there is an essential harmony between the wooden structures and the forest that enfolds them. The atmosphere here is quite different from Ise, in essence the difference between a house and a church. Izumo Taisha is a place of the people, its architecture as robust as the shrines of Ise are fragile and aristocratic. Both are impressive but each reflects a different face of Shinto.

We drove back to Matsue along the north shore of Lake Shinji, the quieter road, and decided to spend the night in a *minshuku* in the small fishing town of Mihonoseki. This is near the tip of the peninsula to the north-east of Matsue. It is a slow drive along the northern shore of the Nakaumi Lagoon, but the narrow road no doubt helps to protect the area from too much commercialisation. The rugged coast here forms part of the Daisen-Oki National Park. At the end of the peninsula is a charming old lighthouse, designed by a French engineer. But the main charm of this area centres on the little town of Mihonoseki, whose quaint back-streets offer a glimpse of an older Japan.

The quay is typical enough of any busy fishing port, but behind the houses that front the water is the old town. At one end, up steep flights of steps, is a large and handsome shrine, again built right against the hillside. We walked along there after supper and the row of lanterns hung under the eaves of the inner shrine glowed softly like a line of mellow moons. This is the oldest shrine in the area after Izumo Taisha and offers special protection to seafarers. From the small market square below the shrine steps, a narrow, roughly flagged street leads into the heart of the town, other streets little more than alleyways. The main street somehow retained a special character and I was not surprised to learn from our hostess at the *minshuku*, that before the Second World War this had been the *hanamachi*, the flower-street or geisha quarter of the town. At that time there had been some sixty geisha-san working here.

Although foreigners have long been fascinated by the Japanese geisha, there are many misunderstandings about the geisha world. Though much reduced, it is still active in many parts of

Japan. But small towns such as Mihonoseki can no longer support a geisha quarter, or maybe no longer want one. But since geisha fully established their profession about the end of the eighteenth century, the nature and quality of geisha have varied from place to place. Kyoto still has six active geisha quarters, but each quarter has its own character and style. In towns such as Mihonoseki the geisha-san would have been clumsy butterflies compared to their elegant, highly trained sisters in Kyoto or the best districts of Tokyo. The differences in geisha-san is reflected in the general attitude to the geisha who work in Japan's many hot spring resorts or *onsen*. Be careful in your use of the phrase, 'onsen-geisha'. The implications are not wholly polite. Like all those inner worlds of Japan, the world of geisha-san is complex, ritualised and difficult for the outsider to understand. As surprising as anything is their survival in modern Japan, particularly as since the Second World War all recruits are volunteers. But in the big cities it continues to flourish, though in Kyoto the smaller quarters are shrinking.

The geisha-san are long gone from Mihonoseki. In their narrow street their houses are gradually being replaced with shops and other modern buildings, but the street for the present retains an old-world charm. At the far end and turning towards the hillside there is a pleasing old Buddhist temple with a pretty courtyard garden where a few old tombs are clustered among the clumps of autumn flowers, cosmos daisies and purple *hagi* bright against the grey stone. Running up the hill behind the temple is a sprawling burial ground where old women crouch by tombstones laying out flowers and tiny cups of rice for their ancestors. It is a place of real character with an atmosphere that is becoming rare in Japan. Everywhere now the modern world intrudes. I shall remember Mihonoseki for charming, if fading, echoes of an older Japanese provincial life.

When the weather is clear, Mt Daisen, 1711 m high and the biggest mountain in western Honshu, dominates the views all around this area. Seen from the west it is an enormous cone and from this has come to be called 'the Fuji of Hoki'. Its other aspects are equally massive but more rugged. We stayed one night near the foot of Mt Daisen. We were lucky enough to find a genuine farmhouse *minshuku*. We arrived rather late and received a slightly surly welcome from the young host who reluctantly moved a van so we could park our car. As we went up to our rooms we heard the sound of a noisy meal in progress in the main room. Our rooms were small and spartan, and the other rooms seemed to be occupied by a construction team whose equipment was scattered everywhere. We began to wonder if we would be welcome here and I felt slightly like an intruder as we were summoned to come down and eat. I need not have worried. We sat at our table and almost immediately the most elderly man in the construction team welcomed us. He looked an exceptionally fit fifty-five, but he told us he was seventy-one. He had grown bored with retirement and also found that work kept him healthy. He managed to get a series of temporary jobs with surveying teams. This group was involved with the planning of a new motorway. The elderly man's warmth thawed out everyone, including our young host and he set off an enjoyable general conversation while we ate our way through a generous do-it-yourself barbecue.

Once the barriers are down most Japanese are very sociable. That is the pleasure of the simpler *minshuku* where one can meet Japanese on their own ground, a bridge across that ever-present gap that keeps the foreigner apart. One also meets a variety of Japanese people one would be unlikely to meet elsewhere. I can still picture that old man, glowing with health and vitality from his red-bronzed face to his crisp grey hair. He told us about his life and his family and his simple philosophy of life. Such people show the best kind of equality in Japanese life. Although a most unpretentious person, he spoke with confidence, even eloquence, and was so natural and charming, gently teasing me while pressing me to more beer. If I had been told he occupied some much more senior position in the road construction company, I would easily have believed it.

We drove across Japan to Hiroshima. What can one say afresh about that tragic city, the site of the world's first atomic bombing, and now inextricably mixed up with Japanese pacifism and the international anti-nuclear movement? I had been to Hiroshima once before in 1972. The visit had left me with ambivalent feelings. The main purpose of this present tour of Chugoku was to go there again to check those earlier reactions. Obviously, it is a sensitive subject. How can one devise a suitable memorial for a human disaster of this enormity, a memorial that does justice to both past, present and future?

The Peace Park is in the centre of Hiroshima, now enclosed by the new and flourishing city that has been rebuilt since the war. At one end of the park, at the epicentre of the explosion, stands the famous skeletal-domed building which survived the blast (Plate 25), the most effective reminder of 6 August 1945 and the death of about 200,000 people within this area. In the centre of the park is a simple memorial arch, and at the other end is the museum of the atomic bombing. Inevitably, as the years pass, the park takes on the air of a sightseeing spot with children feeding the pigeons, amateur photographers jostling for the best views, and ice-cream vendors lined up under the trees. There are other memorials within the park, some gifts from foreign countries. Britain has contributed two beds of roses. Apart from these physical memorials, Hiroshima has elected itself a centre of world peace, a role fostered by wordy conferences and perorations from local leaders. Around the central memorial arch there is at least a little positive action. Young volunteers stand with tins collecting money to provide medical treatment for the remaining Hiroshima victims, denied them by the Japanese government. The rattle of those tins is perhaps the best reminder of the human condition that brings about atomic bombing, and it was the only thing in the Peace Park that stirred real emotion in me.

It would be impossible to underrate the suffering, or the significance of that first bomb, but somehow Hiroshima misrepresents that terrible moment in history and, in doing so, diminishes it, not only for the Japanese but for everyone. The museum is well laid out and both the photographs and the relics of the disaster are horrifying. But the story they tell seems incomplete, with an underlying note of self-pity. The bombing of Hiroshima was not some isolated act perpetrated by the Americans on a wholly innocent people. But a young visitor to the museum might easily form that impression. The bombing belongs within its proper context, for the context carries a warning for the future just as much as the bomb. It would be seen more realistically as the last 'atrocity' in a chain of atrocities: the atrocities of Japan in Korea, in Manchuria, in China and throughout South-East Asia during the Second World War. In simplest terms, had the Japanese stayed out of the Second World War, neither Hiroshima nor Nagasaki would have been bombed. The museum would present a more significant story if that and other simple facts were stated as a background to the culminating horror of the bomb.

Only this year, on the anniversary of the bombing, my Japanese newspaper reported a story that the probable massacre of 300,000 people by Japanese troops in one Chinese town during the Second World War had just been unearthed. At Hiroshima I detect elements of propaganda and self-pity which, in an unpleasant way, trivialise the holocaust they are supposed to be commemorating. War is terrible whether you are burnt to death in Hiroshima or decapitated in a Japanese prisoner of war camp. Such an event demands facing the whole truth.

I do not think the effects of the memorials at Hiroshima are necessarily intentional. For various reasons, in public the Japanese find it difficult to deal with big events or strong emotions and I often notice how such things tend to be trivialised. Most Japanese live on a small scale, physically, mentally and emotionally. A year or two ago Mazda published privately an intriguing book called *The Compact Culture*. Through cleverly chosen photographs of traditional objects the book showed how in various ways the Japanese have long had a deep liking for the small-scale and compactness. This was shown through such things as *bonsai* and miniature tray-gardens, the intricacies of all the domestic objects that stack or fold and the carefully circumscribed interior architecture of *tatami* mats and sliding screens. It was a fascinating study as far as it went, but it failed to follow up the more interesting psychological implications and what might have been the last chapter, 'The Compact Mind'.

Two phrases regularly punctuate my relations with Japanese, 'how charming', and 'how sad'. They may often feel a greater happiness or sadness but the restraints of Japanese life have made it almost impossible for them to express them. I have witnessed a large number of 'peace demonstrations' in Japan and usually they lack the bite of such demonstrations elsewhere. I did not see the worst student riots of the 1960s which were certainly violent, but I have seen big student demonstrations in Tokyo. Superficially the demonstrators seemed dangerously angry, but as one watched for some time the riot seemed to be transformed into an extra-ordinary ritual dance between the rioters and the riot police, with an underlying orchestration which made it harmless. As the world knows to its costs there is a fanatical, radical element in Japan's 'Red Army' certainly capable of extreme action, but these few people are unrepresentative of the general mood or temperament of the Japanese nation.

Of Japanese post-war pacifism as a whole, it is difficult to be objective and I do not think any answers are to be found at Hiroshima which, as I've already suggested, is rapidly turning into little more than a tourist attraction. I think the ordinary Japanese wishes for peace and is peaceable. At the level of commerce and government, a pacifist stance, first imposed by the American post-war constitution, has proved an undoubted advantage. Japan's economic expansion certainly owes something to their limited expenditure on defence, safe under the American umbrella, but that alone would not have made an economic miracle. Defence expenditure is now increasing, but for a long time to come Japan is militarily powerless without the support of the United States.

The saddest footnote to Hiroshima is the neglect of the surviving victims, who have not been provided with adequate medical treatment and insurance by the government, while the Japanese people as a whole have spurned them and turned them into another minority, discriminated against in a number of ways, from the fear of the hereditary effects of radiation. The Japanese have shown a grave lack of compassion. It has proved easier to accuse the bombers than to take care of the bombed. For all these reasons, the memorial museum at Hiroshima tells a disturbingly incomplete story and the unpleasant feelings left by my first visit were confirmed by my second.

A few kilometres south of Hiroshima is the famous shrine of Miyajima, second of Japan's three classic beauty spots. Although the large shrine, situated on a small island, has a handsome complex of buildings, Miyajima's reputation must largely have been made by the great vermilion *torii* or Shinto ceremonial gateway that rises from the sea in front of the shrine (Plate 5). At high tide it stands reflected in the rippling mirror of the sea. At low tide it rises out of the sandy shore, the lofty cross beams reflected here and there in the surrounding pools, while sight-seers wander through the gateway enjoying the view up to the main shrine. Yet again the surroundings have not been improved in recent years. From one angle through the *torii* one looks across the bay to an obtrusive modern temple on the mountainside, a sanctuary of one of the newer religions. An oblique view to the right frames a large funfair, complete with Ferris wheel. Miyajima is worth a visit. At high and low tide there is something beautiful and impressive about the great *torii* standing isolated on the shore, a symbol of Japan to Japanese and foreign tourists alike.

Few things are more depressing in Japan than the state of its politics. Japan misleadingly applies so many western words to Japanese institutions which bear little resemblance to the original. In superficial ways Japan is a democracy, and certainly considers itself as such. But beneath the political façade, the controlling forces are far from democratic. I often think of Japan more as a kind of totalitarian benevolent bureaucracy. Some may think this a harsh or even absurd judgement, but 'one man one vote' alone does not create a democratic society, and in the rigidly hierarchical society of Japan I do not see how a true western democracy can flourish.

Since the war the Liberal-Democratic Party has dominated Japanese politics. Its name is one of the travesties of the political scene. Even its own internal organisation and workings are neither liberal nor democratic, let alone its dealings with the nation or the world at large. But in Japanese eyes it is the party which brought about the 'economic miracle' and which continues to offer the nation the best chance of that most precious commodity, security. So it continues to gather a vast majority of the votes, and for years there has been little hope of the other opposition parties achieving power. The main opposition is the Japanese Socialist Party but prolonged lack of, or even real hope of, office has demoralised it into a futile 'talking shop' whose only form of opposition nowadays is occasional constitutional obstruction. Like so many opposition parties it is richer in criticism than realistic alternative policies. The smaller parties are Komeito, which originally grew out of a new Buddhist movement; the Japanese Communist Party; and the Democratic Socialist Party. None of these has the slightest chance of office except through coalitions, but the continual power-struggles of the factions within the parties often frustrate coalition. The Liberal-Democratic Party did lose a lot of votes at the last election in 1983 after the verdict of guilty on ex-Prime Minister Tanaka and his refusal to retire from politics. Despite this setback it is hard to see the party being defeated in the foreseeable future.

It is important to realise that politicians, including members of the cabinet, are less important to government than in western democracies. Japan is basically governed by its senior civil servants in each ministry who are permanently employed, exercise enormous power and are openly responsible for creating as well as executing policy. Politicians everywhere are to some extent at the mercy of their experienced and senior civil servants, whether they admit it or not. In Japan, it is said that senior civil servants have a number of ways of isolating obstinate ministers. It is this system that has given strength and continuity to government in Japan since the Second World War. The bureaucratic élite are dedicated, incorruptible, highly intelligent and highly trained and only the most gifted get to the top. During their government service they are poorly paid, but they usually retire around fifty-five and take senior and rewarding jobs in the private sector, which forges links between their former departments and the world of commerce and industry, binding the system together around the hierarchical 'old-boy' network. It is not a true democratic system but it has served Japan well.

Like everyone else in Japan, from gangster to housewife, politicians have their defined area of activity. The senior bureaucrats allow them so much power and so much money to play their political role, rather like ministers in medieval times would give an interfering Emperor large sums of money to build a new garden to distract his mind from their affairs. Most Japanese politicians since the Second World War, including the most successful, have been markedly provincial in outlook. And indeed many of them devote much time to attracting development to their own area which in turn strengthens their position and in many cases no doubt brings in 'income'.

The controversial former Prime Minister, Kakuei Tanaka, is the perfect example of this. His basic strength springs from his enormous popularity in his own constituency in the town of Niigata. For years he used his influence to bring valuable developments to this area and, despite the Lockheed scandal, his own people remain intensely loyal to him. By chance I was in Niigata immediately after he had been found guilty of accepting bribes, and his followers were out in force on every street corner collecting signatures to protest his innocence. I confess that many of these minor 'political agents' looked distinctly like bully-boys, but his popularity at home was unshaken by the verdict, whatever the rest of Japan may have felt. It was from his strength in his own constituency that his power and influence grew turning him first into Prime Minister, then to 'king-maker', and at the same time a vastly rich man.

It is tragic that Tanaka involved himself in scandal and corruption as he is a talented man and one of the few really effective leaders in Japanese post-war politics. He is that rare creature in the higher levels of Japanese life: a self-made man. In a society where you are usually judged and placed by the university you went to, Tanaka went to none. He started work after elementary school. With that background his achievement was extraordinary.

Cynical though it may sound, Tanaka probably made only two mistakes, the second more serious than the first. Japanese public life is riddled with corruption. It is a sad fact but one confirmed by Japanese newspapers every day of the week. There are honest Japanese politicians, both in the upper and lower house, but the phrase 'money politics' is now on everyone's lips and despite the overt and enormous recent examples of political corruption, recent Prime Ministers, including the present one, Mr Nakasone, seem strangely reluctant to do anything except talk about reform. Tanaka's first mistake was to get caught. That is obvious enough. But after that the stubbornness and dynamism that had pulled him to the top may prove his eventual undoing. If, instead of protesting his innocence, right at the start of the court proceedings he had offered the Japanese nation a seeming apology, and maybe payed some part of his real gain to charity or the tax man, the matter might well have been dropped. When the case first came to court some years ago I asked a senior public prosecutor what he thought would be the outcome. He was not personally involved with the case, but he reminded me that the Japanese will go a long way to avoid a confrontation, as much in the courts as in private life. He thought that the courts would go out of their way to avoid convicting him, but that Tanaka must provide them with some kind of way out that would be acceptable to public opinion. But Tanaka has never given an inch of ground and has forced the courts, who had delayed a decision for several years, into a guilty verdict. This brought simmering public indignation to the boil, but I suspect that most Japanese resent Tanaka's arrogance more than his guilt. The appeal will not be heard until 1985 and the verdict of the appeal court should bring interesting results.

In the meanwhile Tanaka remains the controlling political power in Japan, maker and breaker of Prime Ministers through his dominating faction in the Liberal-Democratic Party, a situation unthinkable in any western democracy where even the breath of some slight scandal can topple a British minister. The present Prime Minister, Mr Nakasone, is in an impossible position. He was voted into office on the promise to rid Japanese politics of corruption. But the fact is that he is unlikely to remain in that office without the support of Tanaka. Many Japanese are deeply dissatisfied with the situation, but within the system of Japanese democracy there is little they can do about it.

In the last year or two there has been a growing anxiety in the west that the worst forms of nationalism are growing again in Japan, that there could be a revival of militarism and that through their enormous economic strength the Japanese perhaps threaten a new form of world conquest. These are serious questions which are worth examining, though in truth most answers can be little more than informed speculation. Any prediction about Japan's future, or future intentions, must first take into account Japan's relations with the United States, also the development of China, and to some extent the health of the European economy.

In a limited sense, despite its vast economic growth and already existing 'economic empire', Japan is exceptionally vulnerable. It has virtually no natural resources and is now importing nearly half its food, all the time burdened in everything it does by massive over-population. At present its Self-Defence Force is negligible and it has no nuclear weapons. The economy is dependent on exports. Its real international power is its growing investment abroad which is already so large that if the Japanese economy suddenly collapsed major economies all around the world would suffer.

In theory, if trade friction led to trade war and the United States and Europe raised massive tariff-barriers or a total embargo on Japanese goods, Japan's whole economy would be undermined, not least because home production and the domestic market rest on the foundations of the Japanese export trade. But each year that Japanese goods and Japanese investment penetrate deeper into the heart of the western economy, the more disastrous would such a collapse be for the west. There is every sign that such penetration will continue to increase, interlocking the main industrial economies of the world so tightly that soon no part can be allowed to collapse by the other parts.

Obviously Japan's economic success has given them a growing confidence and a growing feeling that they have a right to a more important role on the international scene. That is natural enough although it is partly their own inability to play that role that has so far kept them on the sidelines. In the last few years the Americans have not only urged the Japanese to increase their defence capacity, but also to come out of their shell and exercise their proper influence in international affairs. I believe that what nationalism there is in Japan tends to fester in isolationism, but could become something positive and valuable working on the international scene. Without doubt, particularly among the extreme right-wing fringe, there are seeds of both nationalism and militarism but at present they appear to have no real influence. The howling 'fascist' loudspeakers at the street corners are largely ignored by the Japanese who almost all, I suspect, regret their presence.

I cannot say that I have ever experienced any evidence of nationalism in the political sense. I have already written of that unique Japanese sense of national identity, but that is psychological rather than political. I have also mentioned that the Japanese have less and less need for foreign advisers and foreign services. I know foreigners who deeply resent this and read the darkest motives into the fact that their former clients have now learned to look after themselves. Yet foreigners, once they have learned to speak Japanese, cease to employ their Japanese-language teachers. It's as simple as that.

Inevitably people ask, 'Have the Japanese changed since the war?' I doubt if they have changed all that much though those over fifty-five must still remember the horrors and near-starvation that the Second World War brought to them. The worst enemy of the Japanese people, then and now, is their frightening capacity for blind obedience, which springs from their unquestioning respect for authority, be it thinly disguised 'quackery' or, more sinister, some form of political adventuring possibly leading to a revival of militarism. I am certain that the majority of Japanese are an exceptionally gentle, unaggressive people who sincerely wish only for economic security and peace. But the social structuring that produces those admirable attributes and ambitions also tends to produce a dangerously obedient society who are always vulnerable to the various forms of dictatorial, military government which took over power early in this century, supported by a tradition of military government in Japan stretching back to the Kamakura period.

And where one finds Japanese striking aggressive poses, be it ill-behaved Japanese tourists, or in Japanese politics, I am convinced that all such Japanese aggression springs from a deep national inferiority complex which remains the mainspring of their efforts in both military and economic struggles for success. Through historical mischance, Japan was thrust too suddenly into the modern world and it still has not achieved an easy relationship with it, however eagerly it continues to embrace every western fashion. Until Japan can find its own natural identity in the modern world, it will remain an uneasy bedfellow and will raise dark fears in the western mind about Japan's motives. More serious than that, it will continue to frustrate its own talent at every level and will not make the contribution to the world of which it is capable.

9

Narrow Rural View

SHIKOKU ISLAND

My first view of Shikoku Island was not quite as I expected it. In Japan one should make generous allowances for the innate modesty and required self-denigration.

'Do you speak English?'

'*Sukoshi* – just a little.'

The speaker often turns out to have done postgraduate work on Virginia Woolf or Neil M. Gunn at some British university. The language can be even more deceptive in Japan than appearances.

'Please do not expect too much. It will be very dull for you. Our town has a narrow rural view.'

My two sons and I had been invited for the Golden Week holiday to Shikoku by one of my student's families and Fumio was busy denigrating her home town. People from the Japanese provinces tend to have an inferiority complex in the face of the modern sophistication of Tokyo and the older traditions of Kyoto. I was already enjoying the thought of those deserted beaches and the empty countryside stretching away to the slopes of the mountains. It sounded perfection.

The hydrofoil crossing to Imabari was beautiful; pine-tufted islands of varying sizes, from mere fists of rock to much larger fishing communities, were scattered across the calm Inland Sea, everything brightened by the late April sun. The boat swerved under the span of a great bridge. Soon three bridges will link Shikoku to Honshu and that, before long, will certainly be the end of any rural view, though it will bring some needed prosperity to Japan's smallest major island. Driving from Imabari to Niihama, I peered from side to side wondering when the urban landscape would end and we should emerge into the countryside. We didn't emerge. All the way down the western coast, along the beaches, stretched huge oil refineries and other industrial furniture. There was a good deal of rice farming, but the patches of small fields were isolated among the houses that stretched away to the mountain slopes. I liked it but it was not what I had expected.

Japanese thinking tends to cling to the past and can take time to catch up with present reality. Perhaps lingering in the past and ignoring the present is pleasanter. In many areas of Japan whole communities have changed rapidly since the Second World War from farming into industrial areas, altering both the landscape and the way of life. Many families now live a double life. I have a friend who lives near Niihama. He has a full-time job in an engineering company but he and his family still cultivate a few fields of rice. The change has been very rapid in these areas, modern life sweeping in like a tidal wave. A number of farmers have made money selling their land, but for many, particularly the older generation, it must have been a difficult period of adjustment trying to match their conservative ways and outlook with the encroaching modern world. The change has broken up both villages and families and many people have left the island to find work in the great industrial centres.

That Golden Week – it could not have been more happily named – we drove around the whole of Shikoku. I have made four other visits to the island and in many ways I think it is the most beautiful and, in places, the most unspoiled part of Japan. Its beauty and remoteness always come back to me in one vivid impression. Down on the east coast, where the road winds high above the sea, a small, steep valley thrusts out to the edge of the water where the waves curl round the gnarled rocks. On the floor of the valley, under the cliff I saw a beautiful old farmhouse and spread out before it were a narrow line of greening rice-fields. Shikoku is farmland and sea and the two were beautifully married in that remote valley.

Shikoku is another place of pilgrimage for the followers of Kobo-Daishi. Dressed picturesquely in white robes, white leggings and mittens and grasping rosary and pilgrim staff, they make the round of the eighty-eight temples associated with the great priest. On foot the pilgrimage takes about sixty days but now the majority undertake it by bus or car. I once did it in a Tokyo department store where I circulated swiftly around eighty-eight symbolic stepping stones, by each of which was displayed an object from that temple, and, at the end of the 'course', was blessed by the high priest of one of the most famous temples. The pilgrims are out in force in springtime and everywhere we went we saw small bands of white figures.

Kochi, in the south of the island, is a pleasant old town. We stayed a night in an old-fashioned inn with elderly servants fussing over our comfort and serving us memorable raw and cooked fish dishes. Shikoku is famous for its excellent fish, reason alone for visiting the island. The following morning we wandered up and down the long main street with its intriguing street-market, the stalls laden with mountains of fresh vegetables, mounds of practical-looking country clothing and the occasional antique stall. Half-way down the street we all decided to try our hand at *pachinko*, a kind of pinball machine that for years has had a following of millions in Japan with garish and huge *pachinko* parlours in every large street. You sit on a stool and by the hour try to flick metal balls into the high scoring holes. For millions it is a mindless form of release, an alternative to a cigarette or a bottle of beer. Small prizes are awarded for high scores, and at many parlours nearby there is a booth which exchanges the prizes for cash, thus circumventing the gambling laws. The *pachinko* parlours are said to be controlled by the *yakuza* gangs. The only thing we learnt was that it is harder than it looks.

Shikoku in its island isolation has produced its own culture. Amongst its more unusual features have been dogfighting and bullfighting. Near the entrance to Kochi Castle we saw one of the huge dogs, originally bred in Kochi. I heard nothing of dogfights still taking place, but certainly this huge dog was covered in scars which can hardly have been inflicted by the local cats. The bullfighting takes place at Uwajima, on the west coast, six times a year. The test of strength is between two carefully trained and pampered bulls who push with interlocked horns until the loser falls to its knees or turns away. Near Uwajima is some beautiful, wild coast, with huge bays where pearls are cultivated, the floating racks of oysters lifted out of the water from time to time for the shells to be scrubbed clean by workers on covered floating rafts. All around the southern and western coast there are sightseeing spots, underwater observatories, aquariums and the like. One quiet, isolated bay or piece of rocky shoreline at sunset is worth all of these. If you have a car it is not so difficult to get away from the tourist round. Many of the quite major roads in Shikoku are so narrow that one must frequently back down, without dropping a metre into the adjacent rice field, to allow another car to pass. The motoring is slow but at least the big buses cannot follow.

Takamatsu, chief port of Shikoku, is a pleasant and interesting town (Plate 6) and a good starting point for visiting the island, unless you wish to plunge straightaway into the rural view. Yashima has fine views across the Inland Sea and is full of historic memories as the last refuge of the Taira clan before they were finally destroyed by their rivals, the Minamoto, at the end of the twelfth century. The main attraction of the town is the large landscape garden now called Ritsurin Park; what old-fashioned books used to describe charmingly as 'a stroll garden'. Although it does not rank with the great gardens of Kanazawa and Okayama, it is finely landscaped with an unusual spaciousness, its rocks and pine trees not too crowded, and with broad paths leading around the many ponds and artificial waterways.

It is only 33 km by train to Kotohiragu Shrine (often called Kompirasan), one of the most popular shrines in Japan. The shrine buildings are scattered up the side of Mt Zozusan and the visit involves a one-hour walk up the granite steps that lead ever upwards to the Rising Sun Hall, and beyond to the Inner Shrine and marvellous views over the surrounding countryside where small mountains rise out of the plain like huge pepper-pots. I believe that even now you can hire two sturdy porters to carry you up to the shrine, but the vehicle is little more than a mean-sized crate swung from a pole, so you may prefer the walk. The flight of steps leads straight out of the village street and at every level there is reason to pause and examine a different part of the enormous shrine. The last time I was there the sacred stables, a traditional feature of Shinto shrines, contained three horses, two from Hokkaido and, for no apparent reason, one from New Zealand. Further up there was the sound of shouting from behind a fence and an occasional 'thump'. We peered through the fence and to our delight saw six traditionally robed Shinto priests practising *kemari*, Japan's ancient form of football, the ball being made of deerskin. I had never seen it before except in a few early paintings.

Matsuyama is the largest city in Shikoku. Apart from the fact that I probably had the best steak there I have ever eaten, the castle is also interesting and reasonably original with fine views over the city from the upper floor of the donjon. But what fascinated me most was the Dogo Spa, one of the oldest public bathhouses in Japan. If that were not enough, behind the main bathhouse called *Shinrokaku*, a special bathhouse was built for the Imperial family in 1899, a building of Roman luxury, including a water closet of subdued but Imperial grandeur. The *sento*, or public bathhouse, remains a vital feature of Japanese life. The Japanese treat the bath with the same respect as the hippopotamus. They are a nation of evening wallowers and, in the winter particularly, it is a most civilised habit. The actual ablutions, hairwashing and other intimate attentions are all carried out before entering the bath, perched these days on a rickety plastic stool with lavish supplies of hot water from taps and showers. When every square centimetre of the body is polished and pristine, the moment for the bath has come. Beware. The water may be near-boiling. The technique is to slip straight in up to the neck and remain absolutely still during a few minutes of acclimatisation. From then on you enter paradise.

Most houses in Japan have their own *o-furo*, or Japanese-style bathroom, but it is expensive to heat a deep bath of water every night. Many student lodgings and poorer houses do not have a bathroom, or a shower, so the local *sento* does a roaring trade from about five o'clock onwards, remaining open until around mid-night. The bigger and more modern *sento* offer, besides the basic facilities, sulphur baths, electrified baths and ice-cold dips and other refinements. There was a time when bathing everywhere was mixed. The Meiji authorities put a stop to this out of respect to western prudery about nudity which the Japanese then had no feeling about, and today it is segregated bathing. After the Americans, led by Commodore Perry, had 'invaded' Japan and forced it to open its doors to the west, Congress published an illustrated and huge report on Perry's expedition. All copies of the book are now rare but collectors are most eager for those copies which still contain the famous plate illustrating a Japanese bath-house with mixed bathing. I was forced, regretfully, to give up visiting my local *sento* after my elder son, a keen photographer, had gone along one evening bent on recording life in the raw.

In areas such as Shikoku you touch the 'rice roots' of Japan, that innate and deep Japanese conservatism which no doubt was what my friend really meant by the 'narrow rural view'. All farmers are conservative. Rice farmers are more conservative than most, and despite the post-war urbanisation of so much of Japan, the older inhabitants of these areas are still rice farmers at heart. I happen to know a number of families from Shikoku. The most striking fact about this small group is the great difference in attitude between the parents, now all in their fifties and sixties, and their children in their late twenties and thirties. On occasion I have seen this generation-gap lead to great friction.

Like all people still close to their rural origins, many Japanese attitudes are rooted in the changing seasons and the effects of weather. Today many of these seem rather unrealistic, for many of these attitudes, and certain festivals, belong to the old lunar calendar. With the adoption of the Gregorian calendar in 1873 Japanese seasonal thinking became slightly unsynchronised with reality, though an investigation after the Second World War revealed that 60 per cent of farming communities still followed the old calendars and celebrated annual ceremonies in accordance with them. Formerly, early in February on the eve of *Risshun* (the first day of spring), the New Year of the old calendar, each house was purged of evil spirits by scattering beans. At about the same time Japan's harbinger of spring, the sweet-scented plum blossom, breaks, and despite the sharp cold the honey-scented air is a convincing reminder that the season is changing. Everything makes more sense when the New Year and early spring are brought together.

Quite frequently the Japanese are reminded that even in the safety of the modern world they still live close to the forces of nature. Only in the last month we have moved through the last two weeks of a hot and humid summer which by the end of August begins to play on the nerves. The summer heat broke with a typhoon of which one gust of wind removed the roof of my neighbours' carport, to be followed by two torrential rainstorms that flooded my garden for several hours. Only four days ago, while still lying in bed at about 8 a.m. the wooden frame of the house shuddered visibly for fifteen seconds, the longest earthquake I have experienced in Japan and which at its centre near Nagano measured 6.9 on the Richter scale with some loss of life and considerable damage, mainly through landslides. Earthquakes are particularly unnerving at present, following all the predictions, and some scientific indications, that the Great Earthquake of 1923 may be repeated in Tokyo.

Out-of-date attitudes do linger. At the beginning of each summer it is customary to send greetings cards to relations and friends wishing them good health during the summer season, for in Japanese thinking this is the dangerous time of year. This is not hard to understand. In the old days with no refrigeration, no electric fans or air-conditioning, and when mosquitoes and other insects were more troublesome, there were a number of summer illnesses which no longer exist. Such basic ingredients of the Japanese diet as fish and bean curd must have been hard to keep fresh in the old days while malaria and other fevers were common. Certainly the traditional wooden houses were built for summer, catching every breeze in summertime and every icy draught in winter. I have just spent my first year in such a house which has a complexity of sliding wooden shutters, glazed doors, paper doors and screens. Rather like a boat, trimming a screen here or opening up a wooden shutter there, you sail the house through the seasons. I confess that the weather, in the form of seeping cold, can be penetrating in the winter.

Recently I was talking to a friend from Shikoku about her parents. When she said she thought her father might like to move now that he was retired, I asked if it would be more pleasant for her parents to live in the genuinely rural area around Kochi. She said that would be impossible as they must live near the family burial ground in Matsuyama. As eldest son, her father liked to visit his 'ancestors' about once a month. She had also just sent her mother some sweets. When she telephoned, she asked her mother if she had enjoyed them. But her mother had not yet eaten them as first they had been placed on the Buddhist family altar, a present from the daughter to the ancestors. I do not think the daughter was really much interested in either the family graves or offering sweets to her ancestors, though possibly as she grows older she may revert to these beliefs.

In this hierarchical society there is a clear pecking order within the family. In more conservative families the males take priority in everything and elder sisters are suitably respectful and protective, even to a younger brother. In turn the elder sister demands respect from her younger sisters who will never address her by her first name though she may address them in that way. In most modern families this all means little beyond a customary formality, but I have known cases where seniority is enforced and exploited. In most families the boys tend to be spoilt and parental discipline is weakening everywhere, not least because in many cases teenage boys are physically larger and stronger than their parents. Adolescent assault is part of the recent outbreak of juvenile delinquency.

I knew one girl in Shikoku who experienced the full force of traditional parental discipline. She fought long and hard to marry the man of her choice but her parents were against the match.

Eventually her father successfully undermined her confidence, by destroying her group security, threatening to force her to share a glass of water with him. This symbolic gesture would mean that his daughter was from that moment dead in his eyes, something stronger than disowning her. The same ritual of sharing water is practised by a couple just before mutual suicide. I remember years ago in a coffee shop I thought the girl I was with did not want her glass of water. I picked up the glass to drink and she knocked it out of my hand. She had already sipped the water. The Shikoku girl was then hustled into an arranged marriage and during the few months before the wedding was kept a virtual prisoner. All her mail was destroyed, it was impossible to use the telephone in the house and, when they had to go out, her mother always accompanied her to the lavatory lest she make a secret telephone call or escape.

Even among most of the younger generation, particularly those who have never lived abroad, life is divided roughly into 'what you can do' and 'what you can't'. Behaviour considered unconventional can cause a real shock; original thinking can be far worse. Never walk on the bedding, even though you are just about to get into it. Don't send inland mail in an airmail envelope; you will have your letter returned and be fined by the post office. You must not wear a short-sleeved shirt, although it is hot, if it is not officially summer. Never offer anyone a choice of drinks; make the decision for them since a choice will embarrass and confuse them. Life is punctuated with hundreds of such little rules, most of which are second nature to a Japanese and instilled into them from childhood. Last week the little two-year-old boy next door was being scolded with unusual severity by his mother; the first time in a year that I have heard her raise her voice. I met her and her children later in the street and her son was still looking subdued. His mother explained that she had found him walking into the house with his shoes on. He certainly looked as if he was unlikely to do it again and by the time he was six, taking off his shoes would be a reflex action.

Each society makes its own rules. Many Japanese ones are

perfectly sensible within a Japanese context, others have lost their real meaning and are little more than empty ritual, but are still blindly obeyed. If you live obsessed about what the neighbours or other members of your group are going to think, you are unlikely to take either independent or original action. Where this produces social unselfishness it is excellent but Japanese people spend so much of their time being compelled to act unselfishly, they often react by becoming selfish and anti-social if the situation allows. In the old farming communities of Shikoku there were always genuine common purposes to bind the community together, to give real significance to group decisions and group action. Groups lose their reality in high-rise apartments and in urban life.

The rural life also established a tradition of authority and respect for authority. In the individual farmhouse the male head of the family ruled a tiny, but genuine kingdom and, most important, he was there all the time sharing in the work and the family life. He did not leave his farm at seven and return at nine in the evening. Equally, the headman of the village had a necessary authority and the wisdom of his decisions could be judged by everyone. Indeed, he mostly became headman because he was already respected. Today, in Japan there is an unhealthy and unquestioning obedience to anyone who can lever themselves into some position of authority. In the old days only teachers and doctors were given the Japanese title *sensei*, meaning 'teacher' and in a sense 'master'. Today every actor, dentist, graphic designer, yes, even the gas inspector, is treated as, if not actually called, *sensei*.

I had a full dose of authoritarianism when I moved house a year ago. As I was moving from a small modern apartment into a traditional house, nearly everything had to be new. I decided to install a new gas-fired hot-water system and gas radiators. A kind, almost benevolent, man came from the gas company and I explained what I wanted. He then made some suggestions but was amazed when I agreed in principle but asked to see a detailed drawing before I signed the contract. I was questioning his authority, plus the fact that he was used to dealing with Japanese housewives, some of whom would not have known the difference between a safety-valve and a hot-water tap. It was the same all along the line. In Japan much of the time you are expected to buy from catalogues with minute pictures. There is not the space to hold large stocks. In that week I met the gas-stove-*sensei*, the carpet-*sensei*, the upholstered-furniture-*sensei* and others. Each time I started to complain that it was hard to make a decision from a postage stamp photograph, I was told in various ways:

'I have sold many of these. Therefore it must be suitable for you.'

In the case of the gas-stove-*sensei* I did rebel. The oven I was considering cost £400, the picture showed nothing and the salesman was not even able to give me the exact measurements. He retreated to the authoritarian position and assured me that the oven had his personal and official imprimatur. I could not resist asking him how many times a week he cooked the dinner.

As I watched the groups of white-clad pilgrims – mostly elderly people – making their devotions at some of Shikoku's famous eighty-eight temples I often wondered exactly what they believed and why they made such pilgrimages. Before I ever came to Japan, I thought of it as one of the few countries where Buddhism was still a great and living faith. What I found was little more than a gorgeously attired corpse. Apart from being the caretakers of the dead, Buddhism now seems to play little part in Japanese life, though there are some devout believers. The majority of priests inherit their office without any sense of vocation. Indeed, many priests are forced into a calling for which they are unsuitable. As a result many of them regard it simply as a profession, and the more fortunate make a good living out of it. Financial scandals among the Buddhist clergy are not uncommon. There are good priests and some temples do good works but these are exceptional. For the most part the faith is as dead as the atmosphere of the temples in which it is housed.

Buddhism came to Japan from China and soon fragmented

into a variety of sects, offshoots of Mahayana or northern Buddhism, this school tending to elaborate both beliefs and ritual. On its first introduction it was an aristocratic faith, but around the twelfth century a simpler faith was introduced by the Jodo sect which became popular with ordinary people. Japanese Buddhism is extremely complicated with its variety of sects and sub-sects, the sects established in Nara differing from those developed in Kyoto, and with a further diversification in later centuries with such reformers as Nichiren, and the introduction of Zen Buddhism to Japan in the Kamakura period. Throughout the medieval period Buddhism was in conflict with the govern-ment, the great monastery of Enryakuji maintaining an army of warrior monks who frequently marched down Mt Hiei into Kyoto to enforce their will on the Emperor. One of Kyoto's first temples, ironically it had been established at Emperor Kammu's command to protect his new city from the evil forces from the north-east.

My own two close experiences of Buddhism both touched and impressed me. I have already described how I lived for a year in a small Zen sub-temple in Kyoto. In that household I found every-thing that is best in Buddhism: tolerance, a love of nature, simplicity and kindness. Without doubt there must be hundreds of similar small temples scattered around Japan, in a quiet way offering encouragement and comfort to those around them. In fairness, one must add that the enclosed nature of society make such things as social work, or even simple good works, difficult. Until recently, problems were hidden within the family who too often were not qualified to cope with them. In the last few years the problems of the disabled and the mentally retarded, and now the growing problems of the elderly who are without families, are being brought out into the open and many Japanese are beginning to do admirable volunteer work, now that society is accepting the fact that sometimes it is essential 'to interfere' in other people's lives. Individually, most Japanese are compassionate people, and kind, but they have been brought up to hide their own feelings and respect other people's, which has raised more barriers than was perhaps intended.

Since I first came to Japan I was, like many foreigners, fascinated by Zen. It has exercised an enormous influence on Japanese life and the arts, and has received much publicity abroad. The more I read about it, the more I became convinced that one could only begin to understand Zen by experiencing it, however briefly. So about ten years ago I asked some Japanese friends if they could arrange for me to spend a few days living in a proper Zen training monastery. They arranged for me to go to the large Soto sect monastery of Sojiji where young Soto monks from all over Japan come for six years of basic training. Soto is the second-largest Zen sect in Japan, the Rinzai sect being the largest.

I remember that mid-December day when my friends took me to Sojiji. They were worldly businessmen and also probably had a clearer idea of what lay ahead of me in the next week than I had. It was obvious that they thought I was mad. Sojiji, on the outskirts of Yokohama, is huge with about 300 monks in training. I was taken to see the abbot who explained, somewhat severely, that there was still time to change my mind, but once I set foot inside the monastery, I must be absolutely obedient until the moment I left. Apart from anything else, my pride would have prevented me from turning back at that moment.

I enjoyed my time at Sojiji except for three physical problems: the appalling cold, lack of sleep and the agony in my left knee from hours of *zazen* seated in the half-lotus position. This was not peculiar to me. Many young Japanese develop serious, if temporary, illnesses undergoing the rigours of Zen training, everything from tuberculosis to piles, until their bodies learn to adjust. Our daily routine was severe. We rose at 3.30 a.m.; *if* you can rise from one threadbare blanket spread on the *tatami*. We washed outside in wooden troughs of icy water, and made our way to the vast temple through the bitter night. I had western warm clothes, but during the two-hour morning service and in the *zendo* or meditation hall, we went barefoot. When the service ended at six o'clock, having sat on our feet immobile for two hours, I limped back to my room which then had to be scrubbed and dusted to my Zen-master's satisfaction; the standards of spiritual spit and polish outshining a guardsman's buttons.

At seven we had breakfast, ample but identical to lunch and supper with vegetable soup, rice and pickles with green tea. You could eat as much as you liked, but once food was in your bowl, not one grain of rice must be left. Mostly we lived in silence and there was a sign language and a ritual for everything. At the end of the meal, with the ingenious use of tea and a slice of radish pickle, each bowl was cleaned in turn with the aid of one's chopsticks and the 'dirty' tea and pickle left in the third and final bowl were swallowed. Everything was then neatly wrapped in a cloth, the knot on the top also securing the chopsticks to the bundle. I was never hungry and was kept busy learning all these new ways of life.

The long day was divided between six forty-minute periods of meditation and work. We scrubbed the monastery, did gardening and a variety of odd jobs. I was given the lavatories to clean, partly because I was the junior and partly because the Zen-master could detect my spiritual pride sticking out in every direction. After each meal we had half an hour of rest and conversation. At around 9 p.m. we went to the communal bath, a vast structure which held thirty or forty monks at a time. I think at my primitive stage of Zen development that hot bath was the nearest my tired mind and body came to attaining nirvana, or *satori*, or whatever. Whatever else I learned from those few days at Sojiji, I saw Zen stripped of the glamour and mysticism it is so often invested with by outsiders. Whatever else, it is a hard grind, the daily routine mundane and the spiritual training tough, and in the first stages agony. My understanding of Zen may not have enormously deepened, but it was made more realistic.

Isolation and Outsiders

KYUSHU AND OKINAWA ISLANDS

I arrived in Kyushu in the grand style. Late one autumn, just as the tourist season was closing, I decided to join an advertised one-week tour of Kyushu with the added attraction of a return by boat through the Inland Sea. When I joined the tour I was amazed to find that because of the late season I was the only member of the group, but despite that a 45-seater bus, together with driver and a young lady, were to transport me around the island. I should explain that the main duty of the uniformed young lady was to stand behind the bus and blow a whistle whenever we were forced to reverse. She did also from time to time give sincere if slightly off-key renderings of Japanese folk songs, always a hazard on group bus travel. There was also a Japanese courier.

The Japanese regard the island of Kyushu as the birthplace of their civilisation. Already in the fourth century there was regular contact with China and Korea, for the west coast of Kyushu is only some 200 km from Korea. In the seventh century the Emperor moved up to the Nara region to found the Yamato court where the influence of mainland culture remained strong. Today, the northern part of the island is an important industrial area centring on the large city of Fukuoka while the rest of the island is a favourite tourist resort with its magnificent scenery, many famous hot-spring resorts and four national parks. Some places leave splendid memories, others linger in my mind for their dreary monkey parks and crocodiles imprisoned in zoo tanks barely longer than themselves. Apart from its natural beauties, I would borrow a popular Japanese saying for Kyushu. 'Don't expect too much, then you won't be disappointed.'

There is nothing disappointing about Mt Aso, the largest

volcanic crater in the world, though not the highest. The main crater is 128 km in circumference. Although the volcano may be some 30 million years old, and at one time or another has erupted lava over a large part of Kyushu, the present form of the great crater may be only some 130,000 years old. This outer crater now encloses five smaller craters, one of which remains active and is the main attraction of the area. This is the crater of Nakadake, 600 m across, belching smoke and frequently hurling molten rocks high into the air with the bowels of the earth rumbling beneath your feet. The day I went there the scene of desolation was made more bleak by a driving rainstorm. Around the mouth of the crater there are small concrete shelters where tourists can take cover if the spewing of rock becomes too violent. It was a harsh, barren place but gave an immediate sense of the great volcanic forces boiling below the earth's crust. I was glad to descend again to a greener landscape.

Kyushu is an island of hot springs and one great resort is in the neighbourhood of Mt Aso: Beppu on the shore of the Inland Sea. It is often suggested that the Japanese passion for hot baths derives from the enormous number of hot springs in Japan where from earliest times the comfort and relaxation of hot water was a gift of nature. The Japanese still flock to spa resorts, some to relax in large pools of spring water, others to stew in sulphur springs and some to be buried to the neck in hot, health-giving mud. The hot spring resorts of Kyushu are particularly famous and popular. Even the monkeys at Beppu have acquired a liking for a hot dip.

Everyone should visit a hot spring resort once and Beppu has it all: hot springs for health, and hot springs for pleasure. The hot springs of Beppu bubble and steam to the surface through 3795 different vents, providing nine types of spring water. Should you require acid-weak vitriol, head for Shin-yu, but if you are more particular and require acid-weak vitriol muriated saline, then it must be Umijigoku. The boiling pond at Chinoike-jigoku will assure you a more than adequate vermilion mud-pack. At resorts of this kind some pools are outdoors, some are little more than large and lavish bathrooms, but some are vast indoor pools decked out in all the finery of an Amazonian rain forest. For many years after the Second World War, before the Japanese discovered 'abroad', the Kyushu resorts, particularly in the warmer southern part of the island, were popular honeymoon resorts. Today any self-respecting bride will demand New Caledonia or, at the very least, Hawaii or Guam.

Nagasaki is today sadly more interesting for its history than the fragmentary remains of its historic past. A visit there is almost more an act of piety for the European than a spellbinding round of sightseeing. The loss of old Nagasaki is also partly due to the destruction of the second atomic bomb to fall on Japan on 9 August 1945, becoming the target only after bad weather altered the original plans. Nagasaki is on the extreme western coast of Kyushu and in the second half of the sixteenth century it became an important port and centre of foreign trade. It was accessible to Korea and China and the Philippines and South-East Asia. It also became the trading port for the early ships from Portugal, Spain and Holland, the first gateway to the western world.

The first foreigners to reach Kyushu and Japan were Portuguese traders in 1543, who introduced firearms to Japan. Saint Francis Xavier arrived with a group of Portuguese Jesuits in 1549, making some half-million converts to Christianity by 1600. The Jesuits brought the first influx of European learning and science to Japan, and in turn studied the language and produced the first foreign dictionary of Japanese. This first period of European-Japanese relations is well recorded in what is now called *namban* art, best known for attractive screens showing the landfall of Portuguese ships at Nagasaki, now objects of enormous value. The Portuguese left small influences on the Japanese language and Japanese cooking which have survived to today.

Christianity made considerable strides in the second half of the sixteenth century, even some lords were converted and the government took a tolerant view of the missionaries. But at the end of the century, partly due to the squabbling among the different missionary orders, Hideyoshi became suspicious of Christianity which appeared to be attracting political power in

Kyushu and, having outlawed Christianity in 1587, in 1597 took more drastic action suppressing a small Christian community in Kyoto and crucifying twenty-six Christians in Nagasaki. Tokugawa Ieyasu, who succeeded Hideyoshi in 1600, tolerated the Christians for the sake of the Portuguese trade, but the arrival of the Dutch traders in 1609 and the English in 1613 complicated the situation as it brought Catholic-Protestant rivalries to Japan. Ieyasu also knew that his main political rival had most support from western Japan where Christianity was strongest and in 1614 the Tokugawa government banned Christianity and expelled the missionaries from Japan.

From then on the persecution of missionary priests and Japanese Christians increased, until in 1639 the Portuguese and Spaniards were expelled from Japan and only the Dutch and the Chinese were allowed limited trading rights out of Nagasaki, the Dutch trading post being confined to the tiny artificial island of Dejima, since destroyed. The English had already given up attempts to establish trade and the Dutch were allowed to stay since they had never made any attempt to proselytise. Thus the Japanese nation entered a period of seclusion from the rest of the world which was to last until the Treaty of Kanagawa in 1854 when two ports were opened to American ships, and soon after commercial treaties were signed with other countries.

Even though the Dutch trading post at Nagasaki was so small – and strictly speaking the Dutch were forbidden all contact with the Japanese except those delegated to look after them – from the late seventeenth century onwards it was Japan's only window on the world and a trickle of scientific and medical knowledge seeped through from Europe, while a series of scientists and scholars such as Kaempfer, Thunberg and Siebold were posted to Dejima and on their return published the first serious books about Japan in Europe. These pioneering researches were not insignificant. Siebold, for example, brought back to Holland over 1000 Japanese trees and plants. Kaempfer's collection of Japanese artefacts was early on swallowed up in the collections of the British Museum, no longer identifiable, but Thunberg's collection, possibly including the first three Japanese prints ever brought to Europe, is carefully preserved and documented in Stockholm. Siebold's vast collection is kept at Leiden.

Sadly, little or nothing of this extraordinary period in Japanese history and the life of the Dutch settlement still remain. A small garden marks the former site of Dejima, but most of it lies under a larger quay where the land was reclaimed. Various churches commemorate the early Christian martyrs, the Oura Catholic Church, built in 1865, being the oldest gothic-style building in Japan. The Glover Mansion, the home of an intrepid and enterprising British merchant, Thomas Glover, who founded a trading house in Nagasaki in 1859, is one of the most attractive places in the city with fine views of the harbour from its lovely garden. It is said to be the inspiration and setting for Puccini's *Madame Butterfly*, but there is no evidence for this. That beautiful opera has, however, been responsible for a great many fantasies and misconceptions about Japan.

About 685 km south of Kyushu lie the islands of Okinawa, sixty in all. The largest is known as Okinawa, with the prefectural capital of Naha at the southern end with the airport. Although Okinawa has developed its own culture and language over many centuries, there is evidence that its ties with Japan go back to at least as far as AD 300 with probable migrations from Kyushu. During the long middle ages the Okinawan islands developed independently, ruled over by petty princes until finally unified in the mid-sixteenth century. By the beginning of the seventeenth century Okinawa had become a vassal state to the Japanese Satsuma clan and was also paying tribute to the Emperor of China while it kept the façade of independence with its own royal family. Under three great national leaders during the seventeenth century there was considerable political and social reform and an independent cultural renaissance, which made the best use of both Japanese and Chinese influences.

By the early nineteenth century more and more European ships began to visit Ryukyu, as it was then called, requesting trading rights and freedom for Christian missionaries. The islanders ceased to resist these requests after Commodore Perry had succeeded in opening up Japan. With the opening of the Meiji period in 1868, the Japanese government wished to centralise all administration and in 1879 Okinawa was made a prefecture of Japan ending any real independence of the former Rikkyu and severing all ties with China. But although Okinawa officially became a prefecture of Japan, and paid penal taxes which its inherent poverty could not support, it did not receive the same benefits and political rights as the mainland prefectures. Without question the people of Okinawa, including those who emigrated to the mainland, were treated as second-class citizens and the islands were severely discriminated against, not least in the pre-war militaristic period. The war and post-war period brought new and appalling problems for these islands. American air attacks destroyed Naha and in the following battle for Okinawa some quarter of a million soldiers and civilians were killed and the economy of the island was obliterated. Then, from the end of the war in 1945, these small islands became pawns in the power politics of the Pacific. The Americans were determined to keep their bases against the threats of China to invade Taiwan and the further threat of North Korea. In 1972 Okinawa was finally returned to Japan.

Such a summary of hundreds of years of history, endeavour and human suffering makes an absurd contrast with my own single visit to Okinawa. Signs of the suffering and the endeavour were still to be seen, but bombs and battlefields had obliterated every trace of Okinawa's history except for a fragmentary gateway, in an enclave of garden. Naha is now a flourishing town, with all that that implies with a few bits of tourist bric-à-brac. We had come for some winter sunshine and had been recommended a hotel on the 'Sun-Moon Beach'. I think it was in its way the worst beach resort I have every stayed at in my life. Exchange 'resort' for 'penal settlement' and you are nearer the mark. The hotel smelt of 'good order and discipline', while the swimming arrangements must have been unique. The beach and sea were beautiful, but 25 m from the shore was a floating barrier, and if that was not a sufficient deterrent, this fence was patrolled from dawn until dusk by a rowing boat and two Japanese gentlemen with whistles. The sea was as unthreatening as the Round Pond in Kensington Gardens, but should a swimmer have the impertinence to venture beyond the proscribed area, he or she was treated to whistling, shouts, imperative orders and, once cornered by the floating security guards, a longish sermon. Only pathetic Japanese honeymoon couples, of which there was a plethora, would have tolerated this gross interference with their basic human rights.

I am told by expert Japanese friends that there is excellent snorkling and scuba-diving on some of the small Okinawan islands although accommodation is primitive. For myself, when I now want sun, sea and surf, I would pay not to go to Okinawa and would pay the extra airfare for the magic of Micronesia. In a book of this kind one is expected to enthuse about everything. But in all honesty I cannot recommend the long and expensive side trip to Okinawa unless you are one of those obsessive travellers who must have been everywhere. You have been warned.

Japan shut itself off from the rest of the world in 1639 and remained isolated until 1854, an enormous period of 215 years. The determination of the Tokugawa government to prevent any foreign intercourse was so strict that shipbuilding in Japan during that period was limited to boats that could navigate only in coastal waters, while any individual attempt to leave the country was punishable with death. It is difficult to compare oriental and western cultures, but in that period of 215 years Japan missed the influences of the European Renaissance, the Age of Enlightenment and the first half of the Industrial Revolution. How can one quantify such a historical amnesia? Imagine an Englishman falling asleep in 1639 and waking up in 1854. And even that comparison is false, for Japan in 1639 was ignorant of many things that an educated Englishman of that year would have known.

To risk a rough generalisation, the Japan that rejoined the world at the urging of America in the 1850s was in European terms both feudal and in the main medieval, and certainly a

wholly agricultural society, whose general standard of living was
in many ways primitive. Let us remember that this was just over a
century ago by the time real modernisation got under way with the
opening of the Meiji period. It is a startling thought as the 'Bullet
Train' hurtles through Japan at 200 km/h. A period of isolation
like that is unique to Japan and still exercises a profound influence on most Japanese attitudes and particularly its international
relations.

How far this long period of isolation has reinforced Japan's
exceptional sense of homogeneity and feeling of uniqueness, it is
hard to say. It has probably in itself heightened such characteristics in the Japanese, and produced new feelings which in their
turn have sharpened the old ones. After the opening of Japan, and
throughout the Meiji period, there was an understandable rush to
modernise Japan, and to eradicate everything from it that the
outside world might interpret as primitive. The desire to get in
line with Victorian prudery led to some bizarre contortions in
Japanese social attitudes, and law. Rural communities have a
robust attitude to such things as sex and nudity. Today, many
Japanese have become distinctly prim while the law still forbids
trading in the beautiful erotic prints by the great Japanese artists
of the eighteenth and nineteenth centuries, now publicly exhibited, admired and traded everywhere else in the world. A
stranger Meiji survival is the law which forbids public exhibition
of pubic hair. In most Japanese business hotels if you put 100 yen
in a slot on your television you can 'enjoy' nasty, sadistic, pornographic movies, many made in the United States. But in every
single frame the pubic hair has been censored, only leaving the
film as sickeningly pornographic as before. Such 'modernisation'
leaves one pining for the more primitive attitudes of old Japan.

The Japanese word for a foreigner is *gaijin*, literally 'a person
from outside'. This word is used nearly all the time and one is
seldom described, as in other countries, by one's nationality.
Once a *gaijin*, always a *gaijin*. Any foreigner wishing to live happily
in Japan must accept that basic fact for there is only one entry to
Japanese society and that is by birth. In many countries around

the world, particularly in the more cosmopolitan cities, one is more or less accepted after a few years. In Japan you may be liked but never accepted. One must remember that apart from Japan's 215 years of isolation, since then until very recently few Japanese have travelled abroad, and the majority of those who have, going in sheltered groups, making no real contact with the countries they visit. Also, the sense of Japanese identity and introversion is so strong, that even Japanese I know, who have lived for three or four years in Europe or the United States, return to Japan surprisingly unaffected by the experience and with a shallow understanding of their host country. But since many Japanese can be so unperceptive about their own country, perhaps this is not so surprising.

Of all the Japanese I have known, many of whom would regard themselves as sophisticated, few are completely at ease in the presence of foreigners. I remember the first time I asked a senior Japanese businessman to stay at our house in England, he was so embarrassed that he retreated into the oblivion of several double whiskies and contributed nothing to the evening but a lot of giggling. With several friends, although I think they like me, I know that I am also an object of curiosity, a potential social risk, possible to deal with only because my eccentric and unJapanese ways are redeemed by what is seen as 'sincerity'. But the situation is changing, particularly as more young people go abroad to work and begin to take a real part in foreign life, and as other young people now travel alone, gaining a real experience of the countries they visit. However, a recent poll taken among the housewives of the New York Japanese community showed depressingly little contact with American neighbours or the American scene.

If isolationism lives on at individual level, it most certainly does at political and international levels. I am always surprised at how Japan enjoys such economic success abroad without seeming to become involved in any deep sense in international life. Until recently they have made a poor showing on the international front, probably because most Japanese politicians are notably provincial and Japan's attitude has been unwisely selfish. A few years ago it made itself extremely unpopular in South-East Asia where it appeared to be exploiting the economies of countries such as Thailand without making a real contribution to those countries, either in helping them to build up their own economies or even by direct foreign aid.

The situation has improved and Japan is realising that foreign aid programmes are in everyone's interest, self-interest included. Their contributions compared to other leading industrial nations are still low, but they are now increasing and are being matched by technical aid which is important in itself, and also because it gives younger Japanese technicians and specialists first-hand experience of third world countries. It is only experiences of this kind and real relationships with foreigners that will slowly but finally bring Japan out of its long period of isolation, an isolation which creates attitudes that are undesirable, even dangerous for Japan and everyone else.

It is often difficult to find out the truth about a situation in Japan since the Japanese tend not to discuss, and often to hide unpleasant facts about Japanese life, one of which is the whole subject of discrimination in Japan, something one could travel around Japan for years and never notice. There are several areas of discrimination in Japan, some so taboo that I have been able to mention them only to two or three of my closest Japanese friends. It was obvious that they disapproved of what goes on, but in their Japanese way they did not want to talk about it. It is this escapist attitude that makes it difficult to come to grips with problems in Japan, and provides authority with plenty of room for doing nothing.

There are three main areas of discrimination in Japan, all different but all to some extent rooted in that overwhelming sense of national identity. The discrimination against those called *burakumin* is the strangest, because these people are pure Japanese. It goes back to the Heian period (794–1185) when the ancestors of these peoples were segregated as unclean since they worked as butchers and makers of leather goods. The segregation continues to this day and the descendants live in ghettoes called *dowa chiku*. These people are 100 per cent Japanese but despite changes in the law and a good deal of government action, they are severely discriminated against, particularly in marriage and employment. It is estimated that there are now about 3 million *burakumin* living in over 5000 *dowa chiku* in Japan, that is 2 per cent of the population. Because of the tight system of identity papers in Japan and because of the ghettoes, it is very difficult for the *burakumin* to hide their identity. The routine investigations carried out before marriage or employment are primarily to make certain that a person is not a *burakumin*.

The prejudice is deep-seated at every level of society. Although many Japanese are struggling to improve the conditions of these people, the government drags its feet, official statistics are notoriously unreliable, *burakumin* are not always equal before the law and it has been difficult for them to get a good education. A famous *burakumin* leader started life thinking he could escape prejudice by joining the *yakuza*, an organised gang of criminals. He soon learned that their prejudice was as strong as everyone else's. As in all systems of discrimination and ghettoes, poverty leads to crime and everyone is happily confirmed in their prejudiced opinions. A great deal is being done to eradicate the prejudice. Until that has been removed there is small hope of real development for the *burakumin*. The process of public education is, however, likely to take a very long time.

Another example of racial discrimination concerns the 650,000 Koreans resident in Japan, some 75 per cent of whom are the second or third generation to live here, their parents or grandparents in many cases having been brought to Japan as forced labour between 1939 and 1945. Many of these people speak only Japanese and have never been to Korea. During the colonial period Koreans were given Japanese nationality, but they were redefined as aliens in 1952. Still today, in every way, they are locked out of Japanese society, legally, politically and socially.

A Korean-Japanese is regarded as an alien; Korean-Japanese must be fingerprinted and carry their alien registration cards at all times or risk being imprisoned for up to one year. Korean-

Japanese cannot register in Japanese family registers, usually only menial jobs are open to them and they are not allowed to vote. Matching these more official discriminations is a continuous social one which Koreans in Japan must put up with from the day they are born. Few Koreans have been successful in big business and mostly content themselves running such small-scale commercial operations as restaurants, pinball parlours and scrapyards, many moving nearer to illegal activities with cabarets and sauna baths, while a large number join the organised crime syndicates. Some have made a name in sport and popular entertainment, but the name they use is never their own Korean name.

Again, it is a complex situation, with those of North and South Korea at odds with each other, the prejudices deeply rooted and little sign of any rapid improvement, though more and more Japanese are taking the Koreans' side and improvements in the nationality laws are being forced on the Japanese government as they must conform with the United Nations' charter to which they are signatories. But fundamentally such discrimination springs from Japan's intensely nationalistic identity, and the problems will not be solved until Japan is imbued with a real spirit of internationalism.

Any kind of international outlook is a long way off. At present the Japanese can hardly look at each other fairly and directly, let alone scan wider human horizons. The third area of prejudice in Japan springs from a strong dislike of nonconformity, a suspicion of things that are different, and the embarrassment caused by both. Quite apart from Christianity, there are a number of minority religions in Japan with considerable membership and these 'outsiders' also make the average Japanese uncomfortable. I have had some personal experience of this ever since I made friends about eighteen months ago with members of my local Tenrikyo church.

Like a number of these minority religions, Tenrikyo was founded in comparatively recent times, and like several others, by a woman. Miki Nakayama was born in 1798 and claimed to have received a revelation from God in 1838 in her birthplace, today's

Tenri, near Nara, now the religion's headquarters. The government interpreted her religious ideas as an attempt at subversive social reform and throughout her life she and her followers were persecuted. In 1887 her followers believe that she passed from her physical existence into a spiritual state within the sanctuary of the great church at Tenri. During ther life she wrote the scriptures of her faith and established the ritual of 'the salvation dance' which is the church's main service. Her faith teaches the existence of one God, 'Lord of Divine Wisdom', and also 'God the Parent'. The government, attempting to impose Japanese conformity, classified Tenrikyo as belonging to Sect Shinto, but the Foundress's followers struggled to remain independent and to preserve her doctrine. Superficial elements of Shinto did creep in but with freedom of religion becoming part of Japan's constitution in 1947, there has been a move by the church to return absolutely to the teachings of the Foundress. Today, Tenrikyo has about 2.5 million followers in Japan, others in various countries around the world and a total of some 16,000 churches.

The churches proselytise vigorously and that led to my first meeting with my good friend, Takahashi-san, and the church of Tenrikyo. One morning my door bell rang and standing there was a bespectacled Japanese in his thirties and two younger companions. They explained who they were and asked permission to explain Tenrikyo to me. Warning them that I was not ripe for any kind of conversion, I said I would be interested to hear about their church, and I invited them in for a cup of coffee. Since then, Takahashi-san has told me that in some years of missionary work, it was the first time he had ever been asked in. That morning I learnt something about both Tenrikyo and Takahashi-san. He spoke excellent English and some years before had hitched around Britain. Like many Japanese he had come to Tenrikyo through ill health, in his case serious trouble with his eyes. He has been attached to one of the larger churches in Kyoto for some years but before long will go to San Francisco to join his Japanese wife who, with her mother, is already running the church there.

Since I met Takahashi-san, I have been to the main monthly

service at the local Kyoto church and been twice to Tenri with him. The second time we went with a group of his university friends to pay our New Year respects and to celebrate the occasion eating rice cakes in one of the vast dining rooms attached to the main church at Tenri. When the architectural complex surrounding the central church at Tenri is completed, it will form the largest religious square in the world. Nearby is the Tenrikyo University which has a celebrated library with many rare Chinese and Japanese books. I have enjoyed all my experiences with Tenrikyo, mostly because the members are always so cheerful and seem to obtain real comfort from their faith. This positive attitude to religion in Japan is rare and refreshing. Certainly the warmth and kindness of Takahashi-san springs from his faith and is a happy advertisement for it.

One thing puzzles me about Tenrikyo. What inspired Miki Nakayama's doctrine and unique 'dance' ritual? Born in a village in the middle of Edo isolation, her life and experience must have been circumscribed. Her faith is free from Shinto or Buddhist influences and, one could imagine, owes something to Christianity, though that seems unlikely. Whenever I put such questions to members of Tenrikyo, not surprisingly they reply that it was all part of her revelation from God. But as I sit watching the fourteen ritual prayer dances which form the monthly service, I feel that she must have drawn on some local inspiration. Tenrikyo has one other distinctly unJapanese quality. Churches and services may be conducted by both men and women who are equal in the sight of 'God the Parent'. While not converted to the Tenrikyo church, I have enjoyed unusual kindness and real friendship among its members. But sadly my other Japanese friends are either perplexed or embarrassed that I should involve myself with such people.

There are other, smaller independent religions in Japan, some founded since the Second World War. Shinto has also spawned a few eccentric sects. More important is the large and powerful organisation of Soka Gakkai, which has developed since 1930 out of Nichiren Buddhism, the only Buddhist sect with a strong tradition of proselytising, and disliked among other Japanese for that. Soka Gakkai now claims some 6 million members, 430,000 members overseas in about fifty countries. It founded the political party, Komeito, in 1964, but separated itself from the party in 1970.

In practice, since Japanese live each in their own tight group, what other people think or believe has little influence on others. And in this rather negative way, Japanese society is reasonably tolerant to its own kind, saving its discrimination for the real outsiders. And even those Japanese who belong to minority groups remain unmistakably Japanese. A Boy Scout in Japan is a Japanese Boy Scout. As I see them going down the road, badged and behatted, pennants flying, I wonder what Lord Baden-Powell would have thought. It would seem that the digestive powers of Japanese society can absorb everything foreign except foreigners.

Select Bibliography

1 FOR THE TRAVELLER

A.J.A.L.T., *Japanese for Busy People*, Kodansha, 1984.
J. Brown & Y. Kmetz, *Exploring Tohoku*, Weatherhill, 1982.
M. Cooper, *Exploring Kamakura*, Weatherhill, 1979.
Japan National Tourist Organisation, *New Official Guide: Japan*, 1975.
I. McQueen, *Japan: A Travel Survival Kit*, Lonely Planet Press, 1981.
J.G. Mosher, *Kyoto: A Contemplative Guide*, Tuttle, 1970.
K. Nagasawa & C. Condon, *Eating Cheap in Japan*, Shufunotomo, 1972.
H.E. Plutschow, *Historical Kyoto*, Japan Times, 1983.
H.E. Plutschow, *Historical Nagasaki*, Japan Times, 1983.
H.E. Plutschow, *Historical Nara*, Japan Times, 1983.
L.P. Roberts, *Japanese Museums*, Kodansha, 1978.
R.Stevens, *Kanazawa*, Kanazawa, 1979.
M. Sutherland & D. Britton, *National Parks of Japan*, Kodansha, 1983.
M. Treib & R. Herman, *A Guide to the Gardens of Kyoto*, Shufunotomo, 1980.
J. Vardaman, M. Garner & R. Virgin, *In and Around Sendai*, Sendai, 1980.

2 FURTHER READING

The Kodansha Encyclopaedia of Japan, 9 vols., Kodansha, 1984.
C.J. Dunn, *Everyday Life in Traditional Japan*, Tuttle, 1969.
T. Matsuoka (Editor), *Japan 1984: An International Comparison*, Keizai Koho Center 1984.

3 INTERPRETATION

R.C. Christopher, *The Japanese Mind*, Pan, 1984.
L. Dalby, *Geisha*, Kodansha, 1984.

T. Doi, *The Anatomy of Dependence,* Kodansha, 1973.

R.A. Miller, *Japan's Modern Myth: The Language & Beyond,* Weatherhill, 1982.

C. Nakane, *Japanese Society,* Tuttle, 1984.

B. Rudofsky, *The Kimono Mind,* Tuttle, 1971.

F.L. Schodt, *Manga! Manga! The World of Japanese Comics,* Kodansha, 1983.

E. Seidensticker, *Low City, High City: Tokyo 1867–1923,* Penguin Books, 1983.

J. Seward, *Japanese in Action,* Weatherhill, 1976.

O. Statler, *Japanese Pilgrimage,* Picador, 1984.

E.F. Vogel, *Japan's New Middle Class,* University of California Press, 1963.

E.F. Vogel, *Japan as Number One,* Harvard University Press, 1979.

J.V. de Wettering, *The Empty Mirror,* Routledge & Kegan Paul, 1973.

E. Wilkinson, *Japan versus Europe,* Penguin Books, 1983.

4 ART & ARCHITECTURE

J. Hillier, *The Uninhibited Brush,* Hugh Moss Publications, 1974.

J. Hillier, *The Japanese Print: A New Approach,* Bell, 1960.

K. Iguchi, *Tea Ceremony,* Hoikusha, 1975.

S. Lee, *A History of Far Eastern Art,* Thames & Hudson, 1970.

J. Lowe, *Japanese Crafts,* John Murray, 1983.

R.T. Paine, *The Art & Architecture of Japan,* Pelican History of Art, 1960.

P.C. Swann, *An Introduction to the Arts of Japan,* Bruno Cassirer, 1958.

S. Tsuji, *Japanese Cooking: A Simple Art,* Kodansha, 1980.

5 JAPANESE NOVELS

Kobo Abe, *The Woman in the Dunes,* Tuttle, 1969.

S. Ariyoshi, *The River Ki,* Kodansha, 1981.

F. Enchi, *The Waiting Years,* Kodansha, 1971.

Y. Kawabata, *The Sound of the Mountain,* Tuttle, 1971.

Y. Mishima, *The Sea of Fertility,* 4 vols., Secker & Warburg, 1972–5.

O. Mori, *The Wild Geese,* Tuttle, 1959.

I. Morris, *The World of the Shining Prince,* Tuttle, 1978. (A brilliant commentary on 'The Tale of Genji' and the Heian period.)

S. Murasaki (trans. E. Seidensticker), *The Tale of Genji*, 2 vols., Tuttle, 1978.

N. Soseki, *Mon*, Tuttle, 1972.

J. Tanizaki, *The Makioka Sisters*, Tuttle, 1973.

T. Yamasaki, *Bonchi*, Methuen, 1984.

6   FOREIGN NOVELS ABOUT JAPAN

M. Chand, *The Gossamer Fly*, John Murray, 1979.

M. Chand, *The Bonsai Tree*, John Murray, 1983.

M. Harris, *Yukiko*, Gollancz, 1978.

F. King, *The Custom House*, Longman, 1961.

F. King, *The Japanese Umbrella* (short stories), Longman, 1964.

J. Melville, *The Ninth Netsuke*, Secker & Warburg, 1982.

Index